GNU Coding Standards

A catalogue record for this book is available from the Hong Kong Public Libraries.

Published in Hong Kong by Samurai Media Limited.

Email: info@samuraimedia.org

ISBN 978-988-8381-41-8

Background Cover Image by https://www.flickr.com/people/webtreatsetc/

Table of Contents

1 About the GNU Coding Standards

The GNU Coding Standards were written by Richard Stallman and other GNU Project volunteers. Their purpose is to make the GNU system clean, consistent, and easy to install. This document can also be read as a guide to writing portable, robust and reliable programs. It focuses on programs written in C, but many of the rules and principles are useful even if you write in another programming language. The rules often state reasons for writing in a certain way.

If you did not obtain this file directly from the GNU project and recently, please check for a newer version. You can get the GNU Coding Standards from the GNU web server in many different formats, including the Texinfo source, PDF, HTML, DVI, plain text, and more, at: `http://www.gnu.org/prep/standards/`.

If you are maintaining an official GNU package, in addition to this document, please read and follow the GNU maintainer information (see Section "Contents" in *Information for Maintainers of GNU Software*).

If you want to receive diffs for every change to these GNU documents, join the mailing list `gnustandards-commit@gnu.org`, via the web interface at `http://lists.gnu.org/mailman/listinfo/gnustandards-commit`. Archives are also available there.

Please send corrections or suggestions for this document to `bug-standards@gnu.org`. If you make a suggestion, please include a suggested new wording for it, to help us consider the suggestion efficiently. We prefer a context diff to the Texinfo source, but if that's difficult for you, you can make a context diff for some other version of this document, or propose it in any way that makes it clear. The source repository for this document can be found at `http://savannah.gnu.org/projects/gnustandards`.

These standards cover the minimum of what is important when writing a GNU package. Likely, the need for additional standards will come up. Sometimes, you might suggest that such standards be added to this document. If you think your standards would be generally useful, please do suggest them.

You should also set standards for your package on many questions not addressed or not firmly specified here. The most important point is to be self-consistent—try to stick to the conventions you pick, and try to document them as much as possible. That way, your program will be more maintainable by others.

The GNU Hello program serves as an example of how to follow the GNU coding standards for a trivial program. `http://www.gnu.org/software/hello/hello.html`.

This release of the GNU Coding Standards was last updated April 23, 2015.

2 Keeping Free Software Free

This chapter discusses how you can make sure that GNU software avoids legal difficulties, and other related issues.

2.1 Referring to Proprietary Programs

Don't in any circumstances refer to Unix source code for or during your work on GNU! (Or to any other proprietary programs.)

If you have a vague recollection of the internals of a Unix program, this does not absolutely mean you can't write an imitation of it, but do try to organize the imitation internally along different lines, because this is likely to make the details of the Unix version irrelevant and dissimilar to your results.

For example, Unix utilities were generally optimized to minimize memory use; if you go for speed instead, your program will be very different. You could keep the entire input file in memory and scan it there instead of using stdio. Use a smarter algorithm discovered more recently than the Unix program. Eliminate use of temporary files. Do it in one pass instead of two (we did this in the assembler).

Or, on the contrary, emphasize simplicity instead of speed. For some applications, the speed of today's computers makes simpler algorithms adequate.

Or go for generality. For example, Unix programs often have static tables or fixed-size strings, which make for arbitrary limits; use dynamic allocation instead. Make sure your program handles NULs and other funny characters in the input files. Add a programming language for extensibility and write part of the program in that language.

Or turn some parts of the program into independently usable libraries. Or use a simple garbage collector instead of tracking precisely when to free memory, or use a new GNU facility such as obstacks.

2.2 Accepting Contributions

If the program you are working on is copyrighted by the Free Software Foundation, then when someone else sends you a piece of code to add to the program, we need legal papers to use it—just as we asked you to sign papers initially. *Each* person who makes a nontrivial contribution to a program must sign some sort of legal papers in order for us to have clear title to the program; the main author alone is not enough.

So, before adding in any contributions from other people, please tell us, so we can arrange to get the papers. Then wait until we tell you that we have received the signed papers, before you actually use the contribution.

This applies both before you release the program and afterward. If you receive diffs to fix a bug, and they make significant changes, we need legal papers for that change.

This also applies to comments and documentation files. For copyright law, comments and code are just text. Copyright applies to all kinds of text, so we need legal papers for all kinds.

We know it is frustrating to ask for legal papers; it's frustrating for us as well. But if you don't wait, you are going out on a limb—for example, what if the contributor's employer won't sign a disclaimer? You might have to take that code out again!

You don't need papers for changes of a few lines here or there, since they are not significant for copyright purposes. Also, you don't need papers if all you get from the suggestion is some ideas, not actual code which you use. For example, if someone sent you one implementation, but you write a different implementation of the same idea, you don't need to get papers.

The very worst thing is if you forget to tell us about the other contributor. We could be very embarrassed in court some day as a result.

We have more detailed advice for maintainers of GNU packages. If you have reached the stage of maintaining a GNU program (whether released or not), please take a look: see Section "Legal Matters" in *Information for GNU Maintainers*.

2.3 Trademarks

Please do not include any trademark acknowledgements in GNU software packages or documentation.

Trademark acknowledgements are the statements that such-and-such is a trademark of so-and-so. The GNU Project has no objection to the basic idea of trademarks, but these acknowledgements feel like kowtowing, and there is no legal requirement for them, so we don't use them.

What is legally required, as regards other people's trademarks, is to avoid using them in ways which a reader might reasonably understand as naming or labeling our own programs or activities. For example, since "Objective C" is (or at least was) a trademark, we made sure to say that we provide a "compiler for the Objective C language" rather than an "Objective C compiler". The latter would have been meant as a shorter way of saying the former, but it does not explicitly state the relationship, so it could be misinterpreted as using "Objective C" as a label for the compiler rather than for the language.

Please don't use "win" as an abbreviation for Microsoft Windows in GNU software or documentation. In hacker terminology, calling something a "win" is a form of praise. If you wish to praise Microsoft Windows when speaking on your own, by all means do so, but not in GNU software. Usually we write the name "Windows" in full, but when brevity is very important (as in file names and sometimes symbol names), we abbreviate it to "w". For instance, the files and functions in Emacs that deal with Windows start with 'w32'.

3 General Program Design

This chapter discusses some of the issues you should take into account when designing your program.

3.1 Which Languages to Use

When you want to use a language that gets compiled and runs at high speed, the best language to use is C. C++ is ok too, but please don't make heavy use of templates. So is Java, if you compile it.

When highest efficiency is not required, other languages commonly used in the free software community, such as Lisp, Scheme, Python, Ruby, and Java, are OK too. Scheme, as implemented by GNU Guile, plays a particular role in the GNU System: it is the preferred language to extend programs written in C/C++, and also a fine language for a wide range of applications. The more GNU components use Guile and Scheme, the more users are able to extend and combine them (see Section "The Emacs Thesis" in *GNU Guile Reference Manual*).

Many programs are designed to be extensible: they include an interpreter for a language that is higher level than C. Often much of the program is written in that language, too. The Emacs editor pioneered this technique.

The standard extensibility interpreter for GNU software is Guile (`http://www.gnu.org/software/guile/`), which implements the language Scheme (an especially clean and simple dialect of Lisp). Guile also includes bindings for GTK+/GNOME, making it practical to write modern GUI functionality within Guile. We don't reject programs written in other "scripting languages" such as Perl and Python, but using Guile is the path that will lead to overall consistency of the GNU system.

3.2 Compatibility with Other Implementations

With occasional exceptions, utility programs and libraries for GNU should be upward compatible with those in Berkeley Unix, and upward compatible with Standard C if Standard C specifies their behavior, and upward compatible with POSIX if POSIX specifies their behavior.

When these standards conflict, it is useful to offer compatibility modes for each of them.

Standard C and POSIX prohibit many kinds of extensions. Feel free to make the extensions anyway, and include a '`--ansi`', '`--posix`', or '`--compatible`' option to turn them off. However, if the extension has a significant chance of breaking any real programs or scripts, then it is not really upward compatible. So you should try to redesign its interface to make it upward compatible.

Many GNU programs suppress extensions that conflict with POSIX if the environment variable `POSIXLY_CORRECT` is defined (even if it is defined with a null value). Please make your program recognize this variable if appropriate.

When a feature is used only by users (not by programs or command files), and it is done poorly in Unix, feel free to replace it completely with something totally different and better. (For example, `vi` is replaced with Emacs.) But it is nice to offer a compatible feature as well. (There is a free `vi` clone, so we offer it.)

Additional useful features are welcome regardless of whether there is any precedent for them.

3.3 Using Non-standard Features

Many GNU facilities that already exist support a number of convenient extensions over the comparable Unix facilities. Whether to use these extensions in implementing your program is a difficult question.

On the one hand, using the extensions can make a cleaner program. On the other hand, people will not be able to build the program unless the other GNU tools are available. This might cause the program to work on fewer kinds of machines.

With some extensions, it might be easy to provide both alternatives. For example, you can define functions with a "keyword" `INLINE` and define that as a macro to expand into either `inline` or nothing, depending on the compiler.

In general, perhaps it is best not to use the extensions if you can straightforwardly do without them, but to use the extensions if they are a big improvement.

An exception to this rule are the large, established programs (such as Emacs) which run on a great variety of systems. Using GNU extensions in such programs would make many users unhappy, so we don't do that.

Another exception is for programs that are used as part of compilation: anything that must be compiled with other compilers in order to bootstrap the GNU compilation facilities. If these require the GNU compiler, then no one can compile them without having them installed already. That would be extremely troublesome in certain cases.

3.4 Standard C and Pre-Standard C

1989 Standard C is widespread enough now that it is ok to use its features in programs. There is one exception: do not ever use the "trigraph" feature of Standard C.

The 1999 and 2011 editions of Standard C are not fully supported on all platforms. If you aim to support compilation by compilers other than GCC, you should not require these C features in your programs. It is ok to use these features conditionally when the compiler supports them.

If your program is only meant to compile with GCC, then you can use these features if GCC supports them, when they give substantial benefit.

However, it is easy to support pre-standard compilers in most programs, so if you know how to do that, feel free.

To support pre-standard C, instead of writing function definitions in standard prototype form,

```
int
foo (int x, int y)
...
```

write the definition in pre-standard style like this,

```
int
foo (x, y)
     int x, y;
...
```

and use a separate declaration to specify the argument prototype:

```
int foo (int, int);
```

You need such a declaration anyway, in a header file, to get the benefit of prototypes in all the files where the function is called. And once you have the declaration, you normally lose nothing by writing the function definition in the pre-standard style.

This technique does not work for integer types narrower than `int`. If you think of an argument as being of a type narrower than `int`, declare it as `int` instead.

There are a few special cases where this technique is hard to use. For example, if a function argument needs to hold the system type `dev_t`, you run into trouble, because `dev_t` is shorter than `int` on some machines; but you cannot use `int` instead, because `dev_t` is wider than `int` on some machines. There is no type you can safely use on all machines in a non-standard definition. The only way to support non-standard C and pass such an argument is to check the width of `dev_t` using Autoconf and choose the argument type accordingly. This may not be worth the trouble.

In order to support pre-standard compilers that do not recognize prototypes, you may want to use a preprocessor macro like this:

```
/* Declare the prototype for a general external function.  */
#if defined (__STDC__) || defined (WINDOWSNT)
#define P_(proto) proto
#else
#define P_(proto) ()
#endif
```

3.5 Conditional Compilation

When supporting configuration options already known when building your program we prefer using `if (... )` over conditional compilation, as in the former case the compiler is able to perform more extensive checking of all possible code paths.

For example, please write

```
if (HAS_FOO)
  ...
else
  ...
```

instead of:

```
#ifdef HAS_FOO
  ...
#else
  ...
#endif
```

A modern compiler such as GCC will generate exactly the same code in both cases, and we have been using similar techniques with good success in several projects. Of course, the former method assumes that `HAS_FOO` is defined as either 0 or 1.

While this is not a silver bullet solving all portability problems, and is not always appropriate, following this policy would have saved GCC developers many hours, or even days, per year.

In the case of function-like macros like `REVERSIBLE_CC_MODE` in GCC which cannot be simply used in `if (...)` statements, there is an easy workaround. Simply introduce another macro `HAS_REVERSIBLE_CC_MODE` as in the following example:

```
#ifdef REVERSIBLE_CC_MODE
#define HAS_REVERSIBLE_CC_MODE 1
#else
#define HAS_REVERSIBLE_CC_MODE 0
#endif
```

4 Program Behavior for All Programs

This chapter describes conventions for writing robust software. It also describes general standards for error messages, the command line interface, and how libraries should behave.

4.1 Non-GNU Standards

The GNU Project regards standards published by other organizations as suggestions, not orders. We consider those standards, but we do not "obey" them. In developing a GNU program, you should implement an outside standard's specifications when that makes the GNU system better overall in an objective sense. When it doesn't, you shouldn't.

In most cases, following published standards is convenient for users—it means that their programs or scripts will work more portably. For instance, GCC implements nearly all the features of Standard C as specified by that standard. C program developers would be unhappy if it did not. And GNU utilities mostly follow specifications of POSIX.2; shell script writers and users would be unhappy if our programs were incompatible.

But we do not follow either of these specifications rigidly, and there are specific points on which we decided not to follow them, so as to make the GNU system better for users.

For instance, Standard C says that nearly all extensions to C are prohibited. How silly! GCC implements many extensions, some of which were later adopted as part of the standard. If you want these constructs to give an error message as "required" by the standard, you must specify '`--pedantic`', which was implemented only so that we can say "GCC is a 100% implementation of the standard", not because there is any reason to actually use it.

POSIX.2 specifies that '`df`' and '`du`' must output sizes by default in units of 512 bytes. What users want is units of 1k, so that is what we do by default. If you want the ridiculous behavior "required" by POSIX, you must set the environment variable '`POSIXLY_CORRECT`' (which was originally going to be named '`POSIX_ME_HARDER`').

GNU utilities also depart from the letter of the POSIX.2 specification when they support long-named command-line options, and intermixing options with ordinary arguments. This minor incompatibility with POSIX is never a problem in practice, and it is very useful.

In particular, don't reject a new feature, or remove an old one, merely because a standard says it is "forbidden" or "deprecated".

4.2 Writing Robust Programs

Avoid arbitrary limits on the length or number of *any* data structure, including file names, lines, files, and symbols, by allocating all data structures dynamically. In most Unix utilities, "long lines are silently truncated". This is not acceptable in a GNU utility.

Utilities reading files should not drop NUL characters, or any other nonprinting characters *including those with codes above 0177.* The only sensible exceptions would be utilities specifically intended for interface to certain types of terminals or printers that can't handle those characters. Whenever possible, try to make programs work properly with sequences of bytes that represent multibyte characters; UTF-8 is the most important.

Check every system call for an error return, unless you know you wish to ignore errors. Include the system error text (from **perror**, **strerror**, or equivalent) in *every* error message resulting from a failing system call, as well as the name of the file if any and the name of the utility. Just "cannot open foo.c" or "stat failed" is not sufficient.

Check every call to **malloc** or **realloc** to see if it returned zero. Check **realloc** even if you are making the block smaller; in a system that rounds block sizes to a power of 2, **realloc** may get a different block if you ask for less space.

In Unix, `realloc` can destroy the storage block if it returns zero. GNU `realloc` does not have this bug: if it fails, the original block is unchanged. Feel free to assume the bug is fixed. If you wish to run your program on Unix, and wish to avoid lossage in this case, you can use the GNU `malloc`.

You must expect `free` to alter the contents of the block that was freed. Anything you want to fetch from the block, you must fetch before calling `free`.

If `malloc` fails in a noninteractive program, make that a fatal error. In an interactive program (one that reads commands from the user), it is better to abort the command and return to the command reader loop. This allows the user to kill other processes to free up virtual memory, and then try the command again.

Use `getopt_long` to decode arguments, unless the argument syntax makes this unreasonable.

When static storage is to be written in during program execution, use explicit C code to initialize it. Reserve C initialized declarations for data that will not be changed.

Try to avoid low-level interfaces to obscure Unix data structures (such as file directories, utmp, or the layout of kernel memory), since these are less likely to work compatibly. If you need to find all the files in a directory, use `readdir` or some other high-level interface. These are supported compatibly by GNU.

The preferred signal handling facilities are the BSD variant of `signal`, and the POSIX `sigaction` function; the alternative USG `signal` interface is an inferior design.

Nowadays, using the POSIX signal functions may be the easiest way to make a program portable. If you use `signal`, then on GNU/Linux systems running GNU libc version 1, you should include `bsd/signal.h` instead of `signal.h`, so as to get BSD behavior. It is up to you whether to support systems where `signal` has only the USG behavior, or give up on them.

In error checks that detect "impossible" conditions, just abort. There is usually no point in printing any message. These checks indicate the existence of bugs. Whoever wants to fix the bugs will have to read the source code and run a debugger. So explain the problem with comments in the source. The relevant data will be in variables, which are easy to examine with the debugger, so there is no point moving them elsewhere.

Do not use a count of errors as the exit status for a program. *That does not work*, because exit status values are limited to 8 bits (0 through 255). A single run of the program might have 256 errors; if you try to return 256 as the exit status, the parent process will see 0 as the status, and it will appear that the program succeeded.

If you make temporary files, check the `TMPDIR` environment variable; if that variable is defined, use the specified directory instead of `/tmp`.

In addition, be aware that there is a possible security problem when creating temporary files in world-writable directories. In C, you can avoid this problem by creating temporary files in this manner:

```
fd = open (filename, O_WRONLY | O_CREAT | O_EXCL, 0600);
```

or by using the `mkstemps` function from Gnulib (see Section "mkstemps" in *Gnulib*).

In bash, use `set -C` (long name `noclobber`) to avoid this problem. In addition, the `mktemp` utility is a more general solution for creating temporary files from shell scripts (see Section "mktemp invocation" in *GNU Coreutils*).

4.3 Library Behavior

Try to make library functions reentrant. If they need to do dynamic storage allocation, at least try to avoid any nonreentrancy aside from that of `malloc` itself.

Here are certain name conventions for libraries, to avoid name conflicts.

Choose a name prefix for the library, more than two characters long. All external function and variable names should start with this prefix. In addition, there should only be one of these in any given library member. This usually means putting each one in a separate source file.

An exception can be made when two external symbols are always used together, so that no reasonable program could use one without the other; then they can both go in the same file.

External symbols that are not documented entry points for the user should have names beginning with '_'. The '_' should be followed by the chosen name prefix for the library, to prevent collisions with other libraries. These can go in the same files with user entry points if you like.

Static functions and variables can be used as you like and need not fit any naming convention.

4.4 Formatting Error Messages

Error messages from compilers should look like this:

```
sourcefile:lineno: message
```

If you want to mention the column number, use one of these formats:

```
sourcefile:lineno:column: message
sourcefile:lineno.column: message
```

Line numbers should start from 1 at the beginning of the file, and column numbers should start from 1 at the beginning of the line. (Both of these conventions are chosen for compatibility.) Calculate column numbers assuming that space and all ASCII printing characters have equal width, and assuming tab stops every 8 columns. For non-ASCII characters, Unicode character widths should be used when in a UTF-8 locale; GNU libc and GNU gnulib provide suitable `wcwidth` functions.

The error message can also give both the starting and ending positions of the erroneous text. There are several formats so that you can avoid redundant information such as a duplicate line number. Here are the possible formats:

```
sourcefile:line1.column1-line2.column2: message
sourcefile:line1.column1-column2: message
sourcefile:line1-line2: message
```

When an error is spread over several files, you can use this format:

```
file1:line1.column1-file2:line2.column2: message
```

Error messages from other noninteractive programs should look like this:

```
program:sourcefile:lineno: message
```

when there is an appropriate source file, or like this:

```
program: message
```

when there is no relevant source file.

If you want to mention the column number, use this format:

```
program:sourcefile:lineno:column: message
```

In an interactive program (one that is reading commands from a terminal), it is better not to include the program name in an error message. The place to indicate which program is running is in the prompt or with the screen layout. (When the same program runs with input from a source other than a terminal, it is not interactive and would do best to print error messages using the noninteractive style.)

The string *message* should not begin with a capital letter when it follows a program name and/or file name, because that isn't the beginning of a sentence. (The sentence conceptually starts at the beginning of the line.) Also, it should not end with a period.

Error messages from interactive programs, and other messages such as usage messages, should start with a capital letter. But they should not end with a period.

4.5 Standards for Interfaces Generally

Please don't make the behavior of a utility depend on the name used to invoke it. It is useful sometimes to make a link to a utility with a different name, and that should not change what it does.

Instead, use a run time option or a compilation switch or both to select among the alternate behaviors. You can also build two versions of the program, with different names and different default behaviors.

Likewise, please don't make the behavior of a command-line program depend on the type of output device it gets as standard output or standard input. Device independence is an important principle of the system's design; do not compromise it merely to save someone from typing an option now and then. (Variation in error message syntax when using a terminal is ok, because that is a side issue that people do not depend on.)

If you think one behavior is most useful when the output is to a terminal, and another is most useful when the output is a file or a pipe, then it is usually best to make the default behavior the one that is useful with output to a terminal, and have an option for the other behavior. You can also build two different versions of the program with different names.

There is an exception for programs whose output in certain cases is binary data. Sending such output to a terminal is useless and can cause trouble. If such a program normally sends its output to stdout, it should detect, in these cases, when the output is a terminal and give an error message instead. The -f option should override this exception, thus permitting the output to go to the terminal.

Compatibility requires certain programs to depend on the type of output device. It would be disastrous if ls or sh did not do so in the way all users expect. In some of these cases, we supplement the program with a preferred alternate version that does not depend on the output device type. For example, we provide a dir program much like ls except that its default output format is always multi-column format.

4.6 Standards for Graphical Interfaces

When you write a program that provides a graphical user interface, please make it work with the X Window System, using the GTK+ toolkit or the GNUstep toolkit, unless the functionality specifically requires some alternative (for example, "displaying jpeg images while in console mode").

In addition, please provide a command-line interface to control the functionality. (In many cases, the graphical user interface can be a separate program which invokes the command-line program.) This is so that the same jobs can be done from scripts.

Please also consider providing a D-bus interface for use from other running programs, such as within GNOME. (GNOME used to use CORBA for this, but that is being phased out.) In addition, consider providing a library interface (for use from C), and perhaps a keyboard-driven console interface (for use by users from console mode). Once you are doing the work to provide the functionality and the graphical interface, these won't be much extra work.

Please make your program interoperate with access technology such as screen readers (see `http://www.gnu.org/accessibility/accessibility.html`). This should be automatic if you use GTK+.

4.7 Standards for Command Line Interfaces

It is a good idea to follow the POSIX guidelines for the command-line options of a program. The easiest way to do this is to use `getopt` to parse them. Note that the GNU version of `getopt` will normally permit options anywhere among the arguments unless the special argument '`--`' is used. This is not what POSIX specifies; it is a GNU extension.

Please define long-named options that are equivalent to the single-letter Unix-style options. We hope to make GNU more user friendly this way. This is easy to do with the GNU function `getopt_long`.

One of the advantages of long-named options is that they can be consistent from program to program. For example, users should be able to expect the "verbose" option of any GNU program which has one, to be spelled precisely '`--verbose`'. To achieve this uniformity, look at the table of common long-option names when you choose the option names for your program (see Section 4.9 [Option Table], page 14).

It is usually a good idea for file names given as ordinary arguments to be input files only; any output files would be specified using options (preferably '`-o`' or '`--output`'). Even if you allow an output file name as an ordinary argument for compatibility, try to provide an option as another way to specify it. This will lead to more consistency among GNU utilities, and fewer idiosyncrasies for users to remember.

All programs should support two standard options: '`--version`' and '`--help`'. CGI programs should accept these as command-line options, and also if given as the `PATH_INFO`; for instance, visiting '`http://example.org/p.cgi/--help`' in a browser should output the same information as invoking '`p.cgi --help`' from the command line.

4.7.1 `--version`

The standard `--version` option should direct the program to print information about its name, version, origin and legal status, all on standard output, and then exit successfully.

Other options and arguments should be ignored once this is seen, and the program should not perform its normal function.

The first line is meant to be easy for a program to parse; the version number proper starts after the last space. In addition, it contains the canonical name for this program, in this format:

```
GNU Emacs 19.30
```

The program's name should be a constant string; *don't* compute it from `argv[0]`. The idea is to state the standard or canonical name for the program, not its file name. There are other ways to find out the precise file name where a command is found in `PATH`.

If the program is a subsidiary part of a larger package, mention the package name in parentheses, like this:

```
emacsserver (GNU Emacs) 19.30
```

If the package has a version number which is different from this program's version number, you can mention the package version number just before the close-parenthesis.

If you *need* to mention the version numbers of libraries which are distributed separately from the package which contains this program, you can do so by printing an additional line of version info for each library you want to mention. Use the same format for these lines as for the first line.

Please do not mention all of the libraries that the program uses "just for completeness"—that would produce a lot of unhelpful clutter. Please mention library version numbers only if you find in practice that they are very important to you in debugging.

The following line, after the version number line or lines, should be a copyright notice. If more than one copyright notice is called for, put each on a separate line.

Next should follow a line stating the license, preferably using one of abbreviations below, and a brief statement that the program is free software, and that users are free to copy and change it. Also mention that there is no warranty, to the extent permitted by law. See recommended wording below.

It is ok to finish the output with a list of the major authors of the program, as a way of giving credit.

Here's an example of output that follows these rules:

```
GNU hello 2.3
Copyright (C) 2007 Free Software Foundation, Inc.
License GPLv3+: GNU GPL version 3 or later <http://gnu.org/licenses/gpl.html>
This is free software: you are free to change and redistribute it.
There is NO WARRANTY, to the extent permitted by law.
```

You should adapt this to your program, of course, filling in the proper year, copyright holder, name of program, and the references to distribution terms, and changing the rest of the wording as necessary.

This copyright notice only needs to mention the most recent year in which changes were made—there's no need to list the years for previous versions' changes. You don't have to mention the name of the program in these notices, if that is inconvenient, since it appeared in the first line. (The rules are different for copyright notices in source files; see Section "Copyright Notices" in *Information for GNU Maintainers*.)

Translations of the above lines must preserve the validity of the copyright notices (see Section 5.8 [Internationalization], page 40). If the translation's character set supports it, the '(C)' should be replaced with the copyright symbol, as follows:

©

Write the word "Copyright" exactly like that, in English. Do not translate it into another language. International treaties recognize the English word "Copyright"; translations into other languages do not have legal significance.

Finally, here is the table of our suggested license abbreviations. Any abbreviation can be followed by '*vversion*[+]', meaning that particular version, or later versions with the '+', as shown above. In the case of a GNU license, *always* indicate the permitted versions in this way.

In the case of exceptions for extra permissions with the GPL, we use '/' for a separator; the version number can follow the license abbreviation as usual, as in the examples below.

GPL   GNU General Public License, `http://www.gnu.org/licenses/gpl.html`.

LGPL   GNU Lesser General Public License, `http://www.gnu.org/licenses/lgpl.html`.

GPL/Ada   GNU GPL with the exception for Ada.

Apache   The Apache Software Foundation license, `http://www.apache.org/licenses`.

Artistic   The Artistic license used for Perl, `http://dev.perl.org/licenses/artistic.html`.

Expat   The Expat license, `http://www.jclark.com/xml/copying.txt`.

MPL   The Mozilla Public License, `http://www.mozilla.org/MPL/`.

OBSD   The original (4-clause) BSD license, incompatible with the GNU GPL `http://www.xfree86.org/3.3.6/COPYRIGHT2.html#6`.

PHP   The license used for PHP, `http://www.php.net/license/`.

public domain
           The non-license that is being in the public domain, `http://www.gnu.org/licenses/license-list.html#PublicDomain`.

Python   The license for Python, `http://directory.fsf.org/wiki?title=License:Python2.0.1`.

RBSD   The revised (3-clause) BSD, compatible with the GNU GPL, `http://www.xfree86.org/3.3.6/COPYRIGHT2.html#5`.

X11   The simple non-copyleft license used for most versions of the X Window System, `http://www.xfree86.org/3.3.6/COPYRIGHT2.html#3`.

Zlib   The license for Zlib, `http://www.gzip.org/zlib/zlib_license.html`.

More information about these licenses and many more are on the GNU licensing web pages, `http://www.gnu.org/licenses/license-list.html`.

4.7.2 `--help`

The standard `--help` option should output brief documentation for how to invoke the program, on standard output, then exit successfully. Other options and arguments should be ignored once this is seen, and the program should not perform its normal function.

Near the end of the '`--help`' option's output, please place lines giving the email address for bug reports, the package's home page (normally '`http://www.gnu.org/software/pkg`', and the general page for help using GNU programs. The format should be like this:

```
Report bugs to: mailing-address
pkg home page: <http://www.gnu.org/software/pkg/>
General help using GNU software: <http://www.gnu.org/gethelp/>
```

It is ok to mention other appropriate mailing lists and web pages.

4.8 Standards for Dynamic Plug-in Interfaces

Another aspect of keeping free programs free is encouraging development of free plug-ins, and discouraging development of proprietary plug-ins. Many GNU programs will not have anything like plug-ins at all, but those that do should follow these practices.

First, the general plug-in architecture design should closely tie the plug-in to the original code, such that the plug-in and the base program are parts of one extended program. For GCC, for example, plug-ins receive and modify GCC's internal data structures, and so clearly form an extended program with the base GCC.

Second, you should require plug-in developers to affirm that their plug-ins are released under an appropriate license. This should be enforced with a simple programmatic check. For GCC, again for example, a plug-in must define the global symbol `plugin_is_GPL_compatible`, thus asserting that the plug-in is released under a GPL-compatible license (see Section "Plugins" in *GCC Internals*).

By adding this check to your program you are not creating a new legal requirement. The GPL itself requires plug-ins to be free software, licensed compatibly. As long as you have followed the first rule above to keep plug-ins closely tied to your original program, the GPL and AGPL already require those plug-ins to be released under a compatible license. The symbol definition in the plug-in—or whatever equivalent works best in your program—makes it harder for anyone who might distribute proprietary plug-ins to legally defend themselves. If a case about this got to court, we can point to that symbol as evidence that the plug-in developer understood that the license had this requirement.

4.9 Table of Long Options

Here is a table of long options used by GNU programs. It is surely incomplete, but we aim to list all the options that a new program might want to be compatible with. If you use names not already in the table, please send `bug-standards@gnu.org` a list of them, with their meanings, so we can update the table.

'after-date'

        '`-N`' in `tar`.

'all'   '`-a`' in `du`, `ls`, `nm`, `stty`, `uname`, and `unexpand`.

'all-text'
        '-a' in diff.
'almost-all'
        '-A' in ls.
'append'   '-a' in etags, tee, time; '-r' in tar.
'archive'   '-a' in cp.
'archive-name'
        '-n' in shar.
'arglength'
        '-l' in m4.
'ascii'   '-a' in diff.
'assign'   '-v' in gawk.
'assume-new'
        '-W' in make.
'assume-old'
        '-o' in make.
'auto-check'
        '-a' in recode.
'auto-pager'
        '-a' in wdiff.
'auto-reference'
        '-A' in ptx.
'avoid-wraps'
        '-n' in wdiff.
'background'
        For server programs, run in the background.
'backward-search'
        '-B' in ctags.
'basename'
        '-f' in shar.
'batch'   Used in GDB.
'baud'   Used in GDB.
'before'   '-b' in tac.
'binary'   '-b' in cpio and diff.
'bits-per-code'
        '-b' in shar.
'block-size'
        Used in cpio and tar.

'blocks'   '-b' in head and tail.

'break-file'
              '-b' in ptx.

'brief'   Used in various programs to make output shorter.

'bytes'   '-c' in head, split, and tail.

'c++'   '-C' in etags.

'catenate'
              '-A' in tar.

'cd'   Used in various programs to specify the directory to use.

'changes'   '-c' in chgrp and chown.

'classify'
              '-F' in ls.

'colons'   '-c' in recode.

'command'   '-c' in su; '-x' in GDB.

'compare'   '-d' in tar.

'compat'   Used in gawk.

'compress'
              '-Z' in tar and shar.

'concatenate'
              '-A' in tar.

'confirmation'
              '-w' in tar.

'context'   Used in diff.

'copyleft'
              '-W copyleft' in gawk.

'copyright'
              '-C' in ptx, recode, and wdiff; '-W copyright' in gawk.

'core'   Used in GDB.

'count'   '-q' in who.

'count-links'
              '-l' in du.

'create'   Used in tar and cpio.

'cut-mark'
              '-c' in shar.

'cxref'   '-x' in ctags.

'date'   '-d' in touch.

'debug'   '-d' in make and m4; '-t' in Bison.

'define'   '-D' in m4.

'defines'   '-d' in Bison and ctags.

'delete'   '-D' in tar.

'dereference'
              '-L' in chgrp, chown, cpio, du, ls, and tar.

'dereference-args'
              '-D' in du.

'device'   Specify an I/O device (special file name).

'diacritics'
              '-d' in recode.

'dictionary-order'
              '-d' in look.

'diff'   '-d' in tar.

'digits'   '-n' in csplit.

'directory'
              Specify the directory to use, in various programs. In ls, it means to show directories themselves rather than their contents. In rm and ln, it means to not treat links to directories specially.

'discard-all'
              '-x' in strip.

'discard-locals'
              '-X' in strip.

'dry-run'   '-n' in make.

'ed'   '-e' in diff.

'elide-empty-files'
              '-z' in csplit.

'end-delete'
              '-x' in wdiff.

'end-insert'
              '-z' in wdiff.

'entire-new-file'
              '-N' in diff.

'environment-overrides'
              '-e' in make.

'eof'   '-e' in xargs.

'epoch'   Used in GDB.

'error-limit'
          Used in makeinfo.

'error-output'
          '-o' in m4.

'escape'   '-b' in ls.

'exclude-from'
          '-X' in tar.

'exec'   Used in GDB.

'exit'   '-x' in xargs.

'exit-0'   '-e' in unshar.

'expand-tabs'
          '-t' in diff.

'expression'
          '-e' in sed.

'extern-only'
          '-g' in nm.

'extract'   '-i' in cpio; '-x' in tar.

'faces'   '-f' in finger.

'fast'   '-f' in su.

'fatal-warnings'
          '-E' in m4.

'file'   '-f' in gawk, info, make, mt, sed, and tar.

'field-separator'
          '-F' in gawk.

'file-prefix'
          '-b' in Bison.

'file-type'
          '-F' in ls.

'files-from'
          '-T' in tar.

'fill-column'
          Used in makeinfo.

'flag-truncation'
          '-F' in ptx.

'fixed-output-files'
          '-y' in Bison.

'follow'   '-f' in tail.

'footnote-style'
          Used in makeinfo.

'force'   '-f' in cp, ln, mv, and rm.

'force-prefix'
          '-F' in shar.

'foreground'
          For server programs, run in the foreground; in other words, don't do anything
          special to run the server in the background.

'format'   Used in ls, time, and ptx.

'freeze-state'
          '-F' in m4.

'fullname'
          Used in GDB.

'gap-size'
          '-g' in ptx.

'get'   '-x' in tar.

'graphic'   '-i' in ul.

'graphics'
          '-g' in recode.

'group'   '-g' in install.

'gzip'   '-z' in tar and shar.

'hashsize'
          '-H' in m4.

'header'   '-h' in objdump and recode

'heading'   '-H' in who.

'help'   Used to ask for brief usage information.

'here-delimiter'
          '-d' in shar.

'hide-control-chars'
          '-q' in ls.

'html'   In makeinfo, output HTML.

'idle'   '-u' in who.

'ifdef'   '-D' in diff.

'ignore'   '-I' in ls; '-x' in recode.

'ignore-all-space'
          '-w' in diff.

'ignore-backups'
          '-B' in ls.

'ignore-blank-lines'
          '-B' in diff.

'ignore-case'
          '-f' in look and ptx; '-i' in diff and wdiff.

'ignore-errors'
          '-i' in make.

'ignore-file'
          '-i' in ptx.

'ignore-indentation'
          '-I' in etags.

'ignore-init-file'
          '-f' in Oleo.

'ignore-interrupts'
          '-i' in tee.

'ignore-matching-lines'
          '-I' in diff.

'ignore-space-change'
          '-b' in diff.

'ignore-zeros'
          '-i' in tar.

'include'   '-i' in etags; '-I' in m4.

'include-dir'
          '-I' in make.

'incremental'
          '-G' in tar.

'info'   '-i', '-l', and '-m' in Finger.

'init-file'
          In some programs, specify the name of the file to read as the user's init file.

'initial'   '-i' in expand.

'initial-tab'
          '-T' in diff.

'inode'   '-i' in ls.

'interactive'
          '-i' in cp, ln, mv, rm; '-e' in m4; '-p' in xargs; '-w' in tar.

'intermix-type'
          '-p' in shar.

'iso-8601'
            Used in date

'jobs'   '-j' in make.

'just-print'
            '-n' in make.

'keep-going'
            '-k' in make.

'keep-files'
            '-k' in csplit.

'kilobytes'
            '-k' in du and ls.

'language'
            '-l' in etags.

'less-mode'
            '-l' in wdiff.

'level-for-gzip'
            '-g' in shar.

'line-bytes'
            '-C' in split.

'lines'   Used in split, head, and tail.

'link'   '-l' in cpio.

'lint'
'lint-old'
            Used in gawk.

'list'   '-t' in cpio; '-l' in recode.

'list'   '-t' in tar.

'literal'   '-N' in ls.

'load-average'
            '-l' in make.

'login'   Used in su.

'machine'   Used in uname.

'macro-name'
            '-M' in ptx.

'mail'   '-m' in hello and uname.

'make-directories'
            '-d' in cpio.

'makefile'
            '-f' in make.

'mapped'   Used in GDB.

'max-args'
               '-n' in xargs.

'max-chars'
               '-n' in xargs.

'max-lines'
               '-l' in xargs.

'max-load'
               '-l' in make.

'max-procs'
               '-P' in xargs.

'mesg'   '-T' in who.

'message'   '-T' in who.

'minimal'   '-d' in diff.

'mixed-uuencode'
               '-M' in shar.

'mode'   '-m' in install, mkdir, and mkfifo.

'modification-time'
               '-m' in tar.

'multi-volume'
               '-M' in tar.

'name-prefix'
               '-a' in Bison.

'nesting-limit'
               '-L' in m4.

'net-headers'
               '-a' in shar.

'new-file'
               '-W' in make.

'no-builtin-rules'
               '-r' in make.

'no-character-count'
               '-w' in shar.

'no-check-existing'
               '-x' in shar.

'no-common'
               '-3' in wdiff.

'no-create'
          '-c' in touch.

'no-defines'
          '-D' in etags.

'no-deleted'
          '-1' in wdiff.

'no-dereference'
          '-d' in cp.

'no-inserted'
          '-2' in wdiff.

'no-keep-going'
          '-S' in make.

'no-lines'
          '-l' in Bison.

'no-piping'
          '-P' in shar.

'no-prof' '-e' in gprof.

'no-regex'
          '-R' in etags.

'no-sort' '-p' in nm.

'no-splash'
          Don't print a startup splash screen.

'no-split'
          Used in makeinfo.

'no-static'
          '-a' in gprof.

'no-time' '-E' in gprof.

'no-timestamp'
          '-m' in shar.

'no-validate'
          Used in makeinfo.

'no-wait' Used in emacsclient.

'no-warn' Used in various programs to inhibit warnings.

'node'   '-n' in info.

'nodename'
          '-n' in uname.

'nonmatching'
          '-f' in cpio.

'nstuff'   '-n' in objdump.

'null'   '-0' in xargs.

'number'   '-n' in cat.

'number-nonblank'
              '-b' in cat.

'numeric-sort'
              '-n' in nm.

'numeric-uid-gid'
              '-n' in cpio and ls.

'nx'   Used in GDB.

'old-archive'
              '-o' in tar.

'old-file'
              '-o' in make.

'one-file-system'
              '-l' in tar, cp, and du.

'only-file'
              '-o' in ptx.

'only-prof'
              '-f' in gprof.

'only-time'
              '-F' in gprof.

'options'   '-o' in getopt, fdlist, fdmount, fdmountd, and fdumount.

'output'   In various programs, specify the output file name.

'output-prefix'
              '-o' in shar.

'override'
              '-o' in rm.

'overwrite'
              '-c' in unshar.

'owner'   '-o' in install.

'paginate'
              '-l' in diff.

'paragraph-indent'
              Used in makeinfo.

'parents'   '-p' in mkdir and rmdir.

'pass-all'
              '-p' in ul.

'pass-through'
        '-p' in cpio.

'port'   '-P' in finger.

'portability'
        '-c' in cpio and tar.

'posix'   Used in gawk.

'prefix-builtins'
        '-P' in m4.

'prefix'   '-f' in csplit.

'preserve'
        Used in tar and cp.

'preserve-environment'
        '-p' in su.

'preserve-modification-time'
        '-m' in cpio.

'preserve-order'
        '-s' in tar.

'preserve-permissions'
        '-p' in tar.

'print'   '-l' in diff.

'print-chars'
        '-L' in cmp.

'print-data-base'
        '-p' in make.

'print-directory'
        '-w' in make.

'print-file-name'
        '-o' in nm.

'print-symdefs'
        '-s' in nm.

'printer'   '-p' in wdiff.

'prompt'   '-p' in ed.

'proxy'   Specify an HTTP proxy.

'query-user'
        '-X' in shar.

'question'
        '-q' in make.

'quiet'   Used in many programs to inhibit the usual output. Every program accepting
            '--quiet' should accept '--silent' as a synonym.

'quiet-unshar'
            '-Q' in shar

'quote-name'
            '-Q' in ls.

'rcs'   '-n' in diff.

're-interval'
            Used in gawk.

'read-full-blocks'
            '-B' in tar.

'readnow'   Used in GDB.

'recon'   '-n' in make.

'record-number'
            '-R' in tar.

'recursive'
            Used in chgrp, chown, cp, ls, diff, and rm.

'reference'
            '-r' in touch.

'references'
            '-r' in ptx.

'regex'   '-r' in tac and etags.

'release'   '-r' in uname.

'reload-state'
            '-R' in m4.

'relocation'
            '-r' in objdump.

'rename'   '-r' in cpio.

'replace'   '-i' in xargs.

'report-identical-files'
            '-s' in diff.

'reset-access-time'
            '-a' in cpio.

'reverse'   '-r' in ls and nm.

'reversed-ed'
            '-f' in diff.

'right-side-defs'
            '-R' in ptx.

'same-order'
        '-s' in tar.

'same-permissions'
        '-p' in tar.

'save'   '-g' in stty.

'se'   Used in GDB.

'sentence-regexp'
        '-S' in ptx.

'separate-dirs'
        '-S' in du.

'separator'
        '-s' in tac.

'sequence'
        Used by recode to chose files or pipes for sequencing passes.

'shell'   '-s' in su.

'show-all'
        '-A' in cat.

'show-c-function'
        '-p' in diff.

'show-ends'
        '-E' in cat.

'show-function-line'
        '-F' in diff.

'show-tabs'
        '-T' in cat.

'silent'   Used in many programs to inhibit the usual output. Every program accepting
              '--silent' should accept '--quiet' as a synonym.

'size'   '-s' in ls.

'socket'   Specify a file descriptor for a network server to use for its socket, instead of
              opening and binding a new socket. This provides a way to run, in a non-
              privileged process, a server that normally needs a reserved port number.

'sort'   Used in ls.

'source'   '-W source' in gawk.

'sparse'   '-S' in tar.

'speed-large-files'
        '-H' in diff.

'split-at'
        '-E' in unshar.

'split-size-limit'
> '-L' in shar.

'squeeze-blank'
> '-s' in cat.

'start-delete'
> '-w' in wdiff.

'start-insert'
> '-y' in wdiff.

'starting-file'
> Used in tar and diff to specify which file within a directory to start processing
> with.

'statistics'
> '-s' in wdiff.

'stdin-file-list'
> '-S' in shar.

'stop'   '-S' in make.

'strict'   '-s' in recode.

'strip'   '-s' in install.

'strip-all'
> '-s' in strip.

'strip-debug'
> '-S' in strip.

'submitter'
> '-s' in shar.

'suffix'   '-S' in cp, ln, mv.

'suffix-format'
> '-b' in csplit.

'sum'   '-s' in gprof.

'summarize'
> '-s' in du.

'symbolic'
> '-s' in ln.

'symbols'   Used in GDB and objdump.

'synclines'
> '-s' in m4.

'sysname'   '-s' in uname.

'tabs'   '-t' in expand and unexpand.

'tabsize'   '-T' in ls.

'terminal'
            '-T' in tput and ul. '-t' in wdiff.

'text'   '-a' in diff.

'text-files'
            '-T' in shar.

'time'   Used in ls and touch.

'timeout'   Specify how long to wait before giving up on some operation.

'to-stdout'
            '-O' in tar.

'total'   '-c' in du.

'touch'   '-t' in make, ranlib, and recode.

'trace'   '-t' in m4.

'traditional'
            '-t' in hello; '-W traditional' in gawk; '-G' in ed, m4, and ptx.

'tty'   Used in GDB.

'typedefs'
            '-t' in ctags.

'typedefs-and-c++'
            '-T' in ctags.

'typeset-mode'
            '-t' in ptx.

'uncompress'
            '-z' in tar.

'unconditional'
            '-u' in cpio.

'undefine'
            '-U' in m4.

'undefined-only'
            '-u' in nm.

'update'   '-u' in cp, ctags, mv, tar.

'usage'   Used in gawk; same as '--help'.

'uuencode'
            '-B' in shar.

'vanilla-operation'
            '-V' in shar.

'verbose'   Print more information about progress. Many programs support this.

'verify'   '-W' in tar.

'version'   Print the version number.

'version-control'
             '-V' in cp, ln, mv.

'vgrind'   '-v' in ctags.

'volume'   '-V' in tar.

'what-if'   '-W' in make.

'whole-size-limit'
             '-l' in shar.

'width'   '-w' in ls and ptx.

'word-regexp'
             '-W' in ptx.

'writable'
             '-T' in who.

'zeros'   '-z' in gprof.

4.10 OID Allocations

The OID (object identifier) 1.3.6.1.4.1.11591 has been assigned to the GNU Project (thanks to Sergey Poznyakoff). These are used for SNMP, LDAP, X.509 certificates, and so on. The web site http://www.alvestrand.no/objectid has a (voluntary) listing of many OID assignments.

If you need a new slot for your GNU package, write maintainers@gnu.org. Here is a list of arcs currently assigned:

```
1.3.6.1.4.1.11591 GNU

1.3.6.1.4.1.11591.1 GNU Radius

1.3.6.1.4.1.11591.2 GnuPG
  1.3.6.1.4.1.11591.2.1   notation
  1.3.6.1.4.1.11591.2.1.1 pkaAddress

1.3.6.1.4.1.11591.3 GNU Radar

1.3.6.1.4.1.11591.4 GNU GSS

1.3.6.1.4.1.11591.5 GNU Mailutils

1.3.6.1.4.1.11591.6 GNU Shishi

1.3.6.1.4.1.11591.7 GNU Radio
```

```
1.3.6.1.4.1.11591.8 GNU Dico

1.3.6.1.4.1.11591.9 GNU Rush

1.3.6.1.4.1.11591.12 digestAlgorithm
  1.3.6.1.4.1.11591.12.2 TIGER/192

1.3.6.1.4.1.11591.13 encryptionAlgorithm
  1.3.6.1.4.1.11591.13.2 Serpent
    1.3.6.1.4.1.11591.13.2.1 Serpent-128-ECB
    1.3.6.1.4.1.11591.13.2.2 Serpent-128-CBC
    1.3.6.1.4.1.11591.13.2.3 Serpent-128-OFB
    1.3.6.1.4.1.11591.13.2.4 Serpent-128-CFB
    1.3.6.1.4.1.11591.13.2.21 Serpent-192-ECB
    1.3.6.1.4.1.11591.13.2.22 Serpent-192-CBC
    1.3.6.1.4.1.11591.13.2.23 Serpent-192-OFB
    1.3.6.1.4.1.11591.13.2.24 Serpent-192-CFB
    1.3.6.1.4.1.11591.13.2.41 Serpent-256-ECB
    1.3.6.1.4.1.11591.13.2.42 Serpent-256-CBC
    1.3.6.1.4.1.11591.13.2.43 Serpent-256-OFB
    1.3.6.1.4.1.11591.13.2.44 Serpent-256-CFB

1.3.6.1.4.1.11591.14 CRC algorithms
  1.3.6.1.4.1.11591.14.1 CRC 32

1.3.6.1.4.1.11591.15 ellipticCurve
  1.3.6.1.4.1.11591.15.1 Ed25519
```

4.11 Memory Usage

If a program typically uses just a few meg of memory, don't bother making any effort to reduce memory usage. For example, if it is impractical for other reasons to operate on files more than a few meg long, it is reasonable to read entire input files into memory to operate on them.

However, for programs such as `cat` or `tail`, that can usefully operate on very large files, it is important to avoid using a technique that would artificially limit the size of files it can handle. If a program works by lines and could be applied to arbitrary user-supplied input files, it should keep only a line in memory, because this is not very hard and users will want to be able to operate on input files that are bigger than will fit in memory all at once.

If your program creates complicated data structures, just make them in memory and give a fatal error if `malloc` returns zero.

Memory analysis tools such as `valgrind` can be useful, but don't complicate a program merely to avoid their false alarms. For example, if memory is used until just before a process exits, don't free it simply to silence such a tool.

4.12 File Usage

Programs should be prepared to operate when /usr and /etc are read-only file systems. Thus, if the program manages log files, lock files, backup files, score files, or any other files which are modified for internal purposes, these files should not be stored in /usr or /etc.

There are two exceptions. /etc is used to store system configuration information; it is reasonable for a program to modify files in /etc when its job is to update the system configuration. Also, if the user explicitly asks to modify one file in a directory, it is reasonable for the program to store other files in the same directory.

5 Making The Best Use of C

This chapter provides advice on how best to use the C language when writing GNU software.

5.1 Formatting Your Source Code

Please keep the length of source lines to 79 characters or less, for maximum readability in the widest range of environments.

It is important to put the open-brace that starts the body of a C function in column one, so that they will start a defun. Several tools look for open-braces in column one to find the beginnings of C functions. These tools will not work on code not formatted that way.

Avoid putting open-brace, open-parenthesis or open-bracket in column one when they are inside a function, so that they won't start a defun. The open-brace that starts a struct body can go in column one if you find it useful to treat that definition as a defun.

It is also important for function definitions to start the name of the function in column one. This helps people to search for function definitions, and may also help certain tools recognize them. Thus, using Standard C syntax, the format is this:

```
static char *
concat (char *s1, char *s2)
{
  ...
}
```

or, if you want to use traditional C syntax, format the definition like this:

```
static char *
concat (s1, s2)        /* Name starts in column one here */
     char *s1, *s2;
{                      /* Open brace in column one here */
  ...
}
```

In Standard C, if the arguments don't fit nicely on one line, split it like this:

```
int
lots_of_args (int an_integer, long a_long, short a_short,
              double a_double, float a_float)
  ...
```

For `struct` and `enum` types, likewise put the braces in column one, unless the whole contents fits on one line:

```
struct foo
{
  int a, b;
}
```

or

```
struct foo { int a, b; }
```

The rest of this section gives our recommendations for other aspects of C formatting style, which is also the default style of the `indent` program in version 1.2 and newer. It corresponds to the options

```
-nbad -bap -nbc -bbo -bl -bli2 -bls -ncdb -nce -cp1 -cs -di2
-ndj -nfc1 -nfca -hnl -i2 -ip5 -lp -pcs -psl -nsc -nsob
```

We don't think of these recommendations as requirements, because it causes no problems for users if two different programs have different formatting styles.

But whatever style you use, please use it consistently, since a mixture of styles within one program tends to look ugly. If you are contributing changes to an existing program, please follow the style of that program.

For the body of the function, our recommended style looks like this:

```
if (x < foo (y, z))
  haha = bar[4] + 5;
else
  {
    while (z)
      {
        haha += foo (z, z);
        z--;
      }
    return ++x + bar ();
  }
```

We find it easier to read a program when it has spaces before the open-parentheses and after the commas. Especially after the commas.

When you split an expression into multiple lines, split it before an operator, not after one. Here is the right way:

```
if (foo_this_is_long && bar > win (x, y, z)
    && remaining_condition)
```

Try to avoid having two operators of different precedence at the same level of indentation. For example, don't write this:

```
mode = (inmode[j] == VOIDmode
        || GET_MODE_SIZE (outmode[j]) > GET_MODE_SIZE (inmode[j])
        ? outmode[j] : inmode[j]);
```

Instead, use extra parentheses so that the indentation shows the nesting:

```
mode = ((inmode[j] == VOIDmode
         || (GET_MODE_SIZE (outmode[j]) > GET_MODE_SIZE (inmode[j]))
```

```
    ? outmode[j] : inmode[j]);
```

Insert extra parentheses so that Emacs will indent the code properly. For example, the following indentation looks nice if you do it by hand,

```
v = rup->ru_utime.tv_sec*1000 + rup->ru_utime.tv_usec/1000
    + rup->ru_stime.tv_sec*1000 + rup->ru_stime.tv_usec/1000;
```

but Emacs would alter it. Adding a set of parentheses produces something that looks equally nice, and which Emacs will preserve:

```
v = (rup->ru_utime.tv_sec*1000 + rup->ru_utime.tv_usec/1000
     + rup->ru_stime.tv_sec*1000 + rup->ru_stime.tv_usec/1000);
```

Format do-while statements like this:

```
do
  {
    a = foo (a);
  }
while (a > 0);
```

Please use formfeed characters (control-L) to divide the program into pages at logical places (but not within a function). It does not matter just how long the pages are, since they do not have to fit on a printed page. The formfeeds should appear alone on lines by themselves.

5.2 Commenting Your Work

Every program should start with a comment saying briefly what it is for. Example: 'fmt - filter for simple filling of text'. This comment should be at the top of the source file containing the 'main' function of the program.

Also, please write a brief comment at the start of each source file, with the file name and a line or two about the overall purpose of the file.

Please write the comments in a GNU program in English, because English is the one language that nearly all programmers in all countries can read. If you do not write English well, please write comments in English as well as you can, then ask other people to help rewrite them. If you can't write comments in English, please find someone to work with you and translate your comments into English.

Please put a comment on each function saying what the function does, what sorts of arguments it gets, and what the possible values of arguments mean and are used for. It is not necessary to duplicate in words the meaning of the C argument declarations, if a C type is being used in its customary fashion. If there is anything nonstandard about its use (such as an argument of type char * which is really the address of the second character of a string, not the first), or any possible values that would not work the way one would expect (such as, that strings containing newlines are not guaranteed to work), be sure to say so.

Also explain the significance of the return value, if there is one.

Please put two spaces after the end of a sentence in your comments, so that the Emacs sentence commands will work. Also, please write complete sentences and capitalize the first word. If a lower-case identifier comes at the beginning of a sentence, don't capitalize it! Changing the spelling makes it a different identifier. If you don't like starting a sentence with a lower case letter, write the sentence differently (e.g., "The identifier lower-case is . . .").

The comment on a function is much clearer if you use the argument names to speak about the argument values. The variable name itself should be lower case, but write it in upper case when you are speaking about the value rather than the variable itself. Thus, "the inode number NODE_NUM" rather than "an inode".

There is usually no purpose in restating the name of the function in the comment before it, because readers can see that for themselves. There might be an exception when the comment is so long that the function itself would be off the bottom of the screen.

There should be a comment on each static variable as well, like this:

```
/* Nonzero means truncate lines in the display;
   zero means continue them.  */
int truncate_lines;
```

Every '#endif' should have a comment, except in the case of short conditionals (just a few lines) that are not nested. The comment should state the condition of the conditional that is ending, *including its sense*. '#else' should have a comment describing the condition *and sense* of the code that follows. For example:

```
#ifdef foo
   ...
#else /* not foo */
   ...
#endif /* not foo */
#ifdef foo
   ...
#endif /* foo */
```

but, by contrast, write the comments this way for a '#ifndef':

```
#ifndef foo
   ...
#else /* foo */
   ...
#endif /* foo */
#ifndef foo
   ...
#endif /* not foo */
```

5.3 Clean Use of C Constructs

Please explicitly declare the types of all objects. For example, you should explicitly declare all arguments to functions, and you should declare functions to return int rather than omitting the int.

Some programmers like to use the GCC '-Wall' option, and change the code whenever it issues a warning. If you want to do this, then do. Other programmers prefer not to use '-Wall', because it gives warnings for valid and legitimate code which they do not want to change. If you want to do this, then do. The compiler should be your servant, not your master.

Don't make the program ugly just to placate static analysis tools such as `lint`, `clang`, and GCC with extra warnings options such as `-Wconversion` and `-Wundef`. These tools can help find bugs and unclear code, but they can also generate so many false alarms that it hurts readability to silence them with unnecessary casts, wrappers, and other complications. For example, please don't insert casts to `void` or calls to do-nothing functions merely to pacify a lint checker.

Declarations of external functions and functions to appear later in the source file should all go in one place near the beginning of the file (somewhere before the first function definition in the file), or else should go in a header file. Don't put `extern` declarations inside functions.

It used to be common practice to use the same local variables (with names like `tem`) over and over for different values within one function. Instead of doing this, it is better to declare a separate local variable for each distinct purpose, and give it a name which is meaningful. This not only makes programs easier to understand, it also facilitates optimization by good compilers. You can also move the declaration of each local variable into the smallest scope that includes all its uses. This makes the program even cleaner.

Don't use local variables or parameters that shadow global identifiers. GCC's '`-Wshadow`' option can detect this problem.

Don't declare multiple variables in one declaration that spans lines. Start a new declaration on each line, instead. For example, instead of this:

```
int     foo,
        bar;
```
write either this:
```
int foo, bar;
```
or this:
```
int foo;
int bar;
```
(If they are global variables, each should have a comment preceding it anyway.)

When you have an `if-else` statement nested in another `if` statement, always put braces around the `if-else`. Thus, never write like this:

```
if (foo)
  if (bar)
    win ();
  else
    lose ();
```
always like this:
```
if (foo)
  {
    if (bar)
      win ();
    else
      lose ();
  }
```

If you have an `if` statement nested inside of an `else` statement, either write `else if` on one line, like this,

```
if (foo)
  ...
else if (bar)
  ...
```

with its **then**-part indented like the preceding **then**-part, or write the nested `if` within braces like this:

```
if (foo)
  ...
else
  {
    if (bar)
      ...
  }
```

Don't declare both a structure tag and variables or typedefs in the same declaration. Instead, declare the structure tag separately and then use it to declare the variables or typedefs.

Try to avoid assignments inside `if`-conditions (assignments inside `while`-conditions are ok). For example, don't write this:

```
if ((foo = (char *) malloc (sizeof *foo)) == 0)
  fatal ("virtual memory exhausted");
```

instead, write this:

```
foo = (char *) malloc (sizeof *foo);
if (foo == 0)
  fatal ("virtual memory exhausted");
```

This example uses zero without a cast as a null pointer constant. This is perfectly fine, except that a cast is needed when calling a varargs function or when using `sizeof`.

5.4 Naming Variables, Functions, and Files

The names of global variables and functions in a program serve as comments of a sort. So don't choose terse names—instead, look for names that give useful information about the meaning of the variable or function. In a GNU program, names should be English, like other comments.

Local variable names can be shorter, because they are used only within one context, where (presumably) comments explain their purpose.

Try to limit your use of abbreviations in symbol names. It is ok to make a few abbreviations, explain what they mean, and then use them frequently, but don't use lots of obscure abbreviations.

Please use underscores to separate words in a name, so that the Emacs word commands can be useful within them. Stick to lower case; reserve upper case for macros and `enum` constants, and for name-prefixes that follow a uniform convention.

For example, you should use names like `ignore_space_change_flag`; don't use names like `iCantReadThis`.

Variables that indicate whether command-line options have been specified should be named after the meaning of the option, not after the option-letter. A comment should state both the exact meaning of the option and its letter. For example,

```
/* Ignore changes in horizontal whitespace (-b).  */
int ignore_space_change_flag;
```

When you want to define names with constant integer values, use `enum` rather than '#define'. GDB knows about enumeration constants.

You might want to make sure that none of the file names would conflict if the files were loaded onto an MS-DOS file system which shortens the names. You can use the program `doschk` to test for this.

Some GNU programs were designed to limit themselves to file names of 14 characters or less, to avoid file name conflicts if they are read into older System V systems. Please preserve this feature in the existing GNU programs that have it, but there is no need to do this in new GNU programs. `doschk` also reports file names longer than 14 characters.

5.5 Portability between System Types

In the Unix world, "portability" refers to porting to different Unix versions. For a GNU program, this kind of portability is desirable, but not paramount.

The primary purpose of GNU software is to run on top of the GNU kernel, compiled with the GNU C compiler, on various types of CPU. So the kinds of portability that are absolutely necessary are quite limited. But it is important to support Linux-based GNU systems, since they are the form of GNU that is popular.

Beyond that, it is good to support the other free operating systems (*BSD), and it is nice to support other Unix-like systems if you want to. Supporting a variety of Unix-like systems is desirable, although not paramount. It is usually not too hard, so you may as well do it. But you don't have to consider it an obligation, if it does turn out to be hard.

The easiest way to achieve portability to most Unix-like systems is to use Autoconf. It's unlikely that your program needs to know more information about the host platform than Autoconf can provide, simply because most of the programs that need such knowledge have already been written.

Avoid using the format of semi-internal data bases (e.g., directories) when there is a higher-level alternative (`readdir`).

As for systems that are not like Unix, such as MSDOS, Windows, VMS, MVS, and older Macintosh systems, supporting them is often a lot of work. When that is the case, it is better to spend your time adding features that will be useful on GNU and GNU/Linux, rather than on supporting other incompatible systems.

If you do support Windows, please do not abbreviate it as "win". In hacker terminology, calling something a "win" is a form of praise. You're free to praise Microsoft Windows on your own if you want, but please don't do this in GNU packages. Instead of abbreviating "Windows" to "win", you can write it in full or abbreviate it to "woe" or "w". In GNU Emacs, for instance, we use 'w32' in file names of Windows-specific files, but the macro for Windows conditionals is called `WINDOWSNT`.

It is a good idea to define the "feature test macro" `_GNU_SOURCE` when compiling your C files. When you compile on GNU or GNU/Linux, this will enable the declarations of

GNU library extension functions, and that will usually give you a compiler error message if you define the same function names in some other way in your program. (You don't have to actually *use* these functions, if you prefer to make the program more portable to other systems.)

But whether or not you use these GNU extensions, you should avoid using their names for any other meanings. Doing so would make it hard to move your code into other GNU programs.

5.6 Portability between CPUs

Even GNU systems will differ because of differences among CPU types—for example, difference in byte ordering and alignment requirements. It is absolutely essential to handle these differences. However, don't make any effort to cater to the possibility that an `int` will be less than 32 bits. We don't support 16-bit machines in GNU.

Similarly, don't make any effort to cater to the possibility that `long` will be smaller than predefined types like `size_t`. For example, the following code is ok:

```
printf ("size = %lu\n", (unsigned long) sizeof array);
printf ("diff = %ld\n", (long) (pointer2 - pointer1));
```

1989 Standard C requires this to work, and we know of only one counterexample: 64-bit programs on Microsoft Windows. We will leave it to those who want to port GNU programs to that environment to figure out how to do it.

Predefined file-size types like `off_t` are an exception: they are longer than `long` on many platforms, so code like the above won't work with them. One way to print an `off_t` value portably is to print its digits yourself, one by one.

Don't assume that the address of an `int` object is also the address of its least-significant byte. This is false on big-endian machines. Thus, don't make the following mistake:

```
int c;
...
while ((c = getchar ()) != EOF)
  write (file_descriptor, &c, 1);
```

Instead, use `unsigned char` as follows. (The `unsigned` is for portability to unusual systems where `char` is signed and where there is integer overflow checking.)

```
int c;
while ((c = getchar ()) != EOF)
  {
    unsigned char u = c;
    write (file_descriptor, &u, 1);
  }
```

Avoid casting pointers to integers if you can. Such casts greatly reduce portability, and in most programs they are easy to avoid. In the cases where casting pointers to integers is essential—such as, a Lisp interpreter which stores type information as well as an address in one word—you'll have to make explicit provisions to handle different word sizes. You will also need to make provision for systems in which the normal range of addresses you can get from `malloc` starts far away from zero.

5.7 Calling System Functions

Historically, C implementations differed substantially, and many systems lacked a full implementation of ANSI/ISO C89. Nowadays, however, all practical systems have a C89 compiler and GNU C supports almost all of C99 and some of C11. Similarly, most systems implement POSIX.1-2001 libraries and tools, and many have POSIX.1-2008.

Hence, there is little reason to support old C or non-POSIX systems, and you may want to take advantage of standard C and POSIX to write clearer, more portable, or faster code. You should use standard interfaces where possible; but if GNU extensions make your program more maintainable, powerful, or otherwise better, don't hesitate to use them. In any case, don't make your own declaration of system functions; that's a recipe for conflict.

Despite the standards, nearly every library function has some sort of portability issue on some system or another. Here are some examples:

open   Names with trailing /'s are mishandled on many platforms.

printf   long double may be unimplemented; floating values Infinity and NaN are often mishandled; output for large precisions may be incorrect.

readlink   May return int instead of ssize_t.

scanf   On Windows, errno is not set on failure.

Gnulib (http://www.gnu.org/software/gnulib/) is a big help in this regard. Gnulib provides implementations of standard interfaces on many of the systems that lack them, including portable implementations of enhanced GNU interfaces, thereby making their use portable, and of POSIX-1.2008 interfaces, some of which are missing even on up-to-date GNU systems.

Gnulib also provides many useful non-standard interfaces; for example, C implementations of standard data structures (hash tables, binary trees), error-checking type-safe wrappers for memory allocation functions (xmalloc, xrealloc), and output of error messages.

Gnulib integrates with GNU Autoconf and Automake to remove much of the burden of writing portable code from the programmer: Gnulib makes your configure script automatically determine what features are missing and use the Gnulib code to supply the missing pieces.

The Gnulib and Autoconf manuals have extensive sections on portability: Section "Introduction" in Gnulib and see Section "Portable C and C++" in Autoconf. Please consult them for many more details.

5.8 Internationalization

GNU has a library called GNU gettext that makes it easy to translate the messages in a program into various languages. You should use this library in every program. Use English for the messages as they appear in the program, and let gettext provide the way to translate them into other languages.

Using GNU gettext involves putting a call to the gettext macro around each string that might need translation—like this:

```
printf (gettext ("Processing file '%s'..."), file);
```
This permits GNU gettext to replace the string `"Processing file '%s'..."` with a translated version.

Once a program uses gettext, please make a point of writing calls to **gettext** when you add new strings that call for translation.

Using GNU gettext in a package involves specifying a *text domain name* for the package. The text domain name is used to separate the translations for this package from the translations for other packages. Normally, the text domain name should be the same as the name of the package—for example, '**coreutils**' for the GNU core utilities.

To enable gettext to work well, avoid writing code that makes assumptions about the structure of words or sentences. When you want the precise text of a sentence to vary depending on the data, use two or more alternative string constants each containing a complete sentences, rather than inserting conditionalized words or phrases into a single sentence framework.

Here is an example of what not to do:
```
printf ("%s is full", capacity > 5000000 ? "disk" : "floppy disk");
```
If you apply gettext to all strings, like this,
```
printf (gettext ("%s is full"),
        capacity > 5000000 ? gettext ("disk") : gettext ("floppy disk"));
```
the translator will hardly know that "disk" and "floppy disk" are meant to be substituted in the other string. Worse, in some languages (like French) the construction will not work: the translation of the word "full" depends on the gender of the first part of the sentence; it happens to be not the same for "disk" as for "floppy disk".

Complete sentences can be translated without problems:
```
printf (capacity > 5000000 ? gettext ("disk is full")
        : gettext ("floppy disk is full"));
```
A similar problem appears at the level of sentence structure with this code:
```
printf ("#  Implicit rule search has%s been done.\n",
        f->tried_implicit ? "" : " not");
```
Adding **gettext** calls to this code cannot give correct results for all languages, because negation in some languages requires adding words at more than one place in the sentence. By contrast, adding **gettext** calls does the job straightforwardly if the code starts out like this:
```
printf (f->tried_implicit
        ? "#  Implicit rule search has been done.\n",
        : "#  Implicit rule search has not been done.\n");
```
Another example is this one:
```
printf ("%d file%s processed", nfiles,
        nfiles != 1 ? "s" : "");
```
The problem with this example is that it assumes that plurals are made by adding 's'. If you apply gettext to the format string, like this,
```
printf (gettext ("%d file%s processed"), nfiles,
        nfiles != 1 ? "s" : "");
```

the message can use different words, but it will still be forced to use 's' for the plural. Here is a better way, with gettext being applied to the two strings independently:

```
printf ((nfiles != 1 ? gettext ("%d files processed")
         : gettext ("%d file processed")),
        nfiles);
```

But this still doesn't work for languages like Polish, which has three plural forms: one for nfiles == 1, one for nfiles == 2, 3, 4, 22, 23, 24, ... and one for the rest. The GNU ngettext function solves this problem:

```
printf (ngettext ("%d files processed", "%d file processed", nfiles),
        nfiles);
```

5.9 Character Set

Sticking to the ASCII character set (plain text, 7-bit characters) is preferred in GNU source code comments, text documents, and other contexts, unless there is good reason to do something else because of the application domain. For example, if source code deals with the French Revolutionary calendar, it is OK if its literal strings contain accented characters in month names like "Floréal". Also, it is OK (but not required) to use non-ASCII characters to represent proper names of contributors in change logs (see Section 6.8 [Change Logs], page 46).

If you need to use non-ASCII characters, you should normally stick with one encoding, certainly within a single file. UTF-8 is likely to be the best choice.

5.10 Quote Characters

In the C locale, the output of GNU programs should stick to plain ASCII for quotation characters in messages to users: preferably 0x22 ('"') or 0x27 (''') for both opening and closing quotes. Although GNU programs traditionally used 0x60 ('`') for opening and 0x27 (''') for closing quotes, nowadays quotes ``like this'' are typically rendered asymmetrically, so quoting '"like this"' or ''like this'' typically looks better.

It is ok, but not required, for GNU programs to generate locale-specific quotes in non-C locales. For example:

```
printf (gettext ("Processing file '%s'..."), file);
```

Here, a French translation might cause `gettext` to return the string `"Traitement de fichier « %s »..."`, yielding quotes more appropriate for a French locale.

Sometimes a program may need to use opening and closing quotes directly. By convention, `gettext` translates the string '"`"' to the opening quote and the string '"'"' to the closing quote, and a program can use these translations. Generally, though, it is better to translate quote characters in the context of longer strings.

If the output of your program is ever likely to be parsed by another program, it is good to provide an option that makes this parsing reliable. For example, you could escape special characters using conventions from the C language or the Bourne shell. See for example the option `--quoting-style` of GNU `ls`.

5.11 Mmap

If you use `mmap` to read or write files, don't assume it either works on all files or fails for all files. It may work on some files and fail on others.

The proper way to use `mmap` is to try it on the specific file for which you want to use it—and if `mmap` doesn't work, fall back on doing the job in another way using `read` and `write`.

The reason this precaution is needed is that the GNU kernel (the HURD) provides a user-extensible file system, in which there can be many different kinds of "ordinary files". Many of them support `mmap`, but some do not. It is important to make programs handle all these kinds of files.

6 Documenting Programs

A GNU program should ideally come with full free documentation, adequate for both reference and tutorial purposes. If the package can be programmed or extended, the documentation should cover programming or extending it, as well as just using it.

6.1 GNU Manuals

The preferred document format for the GNU system is the Texinfo formatting language. Every GNU package should (ideally) have documentation in Texinfo both for reference and for learners. Texinfo makes it possible to produce a good quality formatted book, using TeX, and to generate an Info file. It is also possible to generate HTML output from Texinfo source. See the Texinfo manual, either the hardcopy, or the on-line version available through `info` or the Emacs Info subsystem (`C-h i`).

Nowadays some other formats such as Docbook and Sgmltexi can be converted automatically into Texinfo. It is ok to produce the Texinfo documentation by conversion this way, as long as it gives good results.

Make sure your manual is clear to a reader who knows nothing about the topic and reads it straight through. This means covering basic topics at the beginning, and advanced topics only later. This also means defining every specialized term when it is first used.

Programmers tend to carry over the structure of the program as the structure for its documentation. But this structure is not necessarily good for explaining how to use the program; it may be irrelevant and confusing for a user.

Instead, the right way to structure documentation is according to the concepts and questions that a user will have in mind when reading it. This principle applies at every level, from the lowest (ordering sentences in a paragraph) to the highest (ordering of chapter topics within the manual). Sometimes this structure of ideas matches the structure of the implementation of the software being documented—but often they are different. An important part of learning to write good documentation is to learn to notice when you have unthinkingly structured the documentation like the implementation, stop yourself, and look for better alternatives.

For example, each program in the GNU system probably ought to be documented in one manual; but this does not mean each program should have its own manual. That would be following the structure of the implementation, rather than the structure that helps the user understand.

Instead, each manual should cover a coherent *topic*. For example, instead of a manual for `diff` and a manual for `diff3`, we have one manual for "comparison of files" which covers both of those programs, as well as `cmp`. By documenting these programs together, we can make the whole subject clearer.

The manual which discusses a program should certainly document all of the program's command-line options and all of its commands. It should give examples of their use. But don't organize the manual as a list of features. Instead, organize it logically, by subtopics. Address the questions that a user will ask when thinking about the job that the program does. Don't just tell the reader what each feature can do—say what jobs it is good for, and show how to use it for those jobs. Explain what is recommended usage, and what kinds of usage users should avoid.

In general, a GNU manual should serve both as tutorial and reference. It should be set up for convenient access to each topic through Info, and for reading straight through (appendixes aside). A GNU manual should give a good introduction to a beginner reading through from the start, and should also provide all the details that hackers want. The Bison manual is a good example of this—please take a look at it to see what we mean.

That is not as hard as it first sounds. Arrange each chapter as a logical breakdown of its topic, but order the sections, and write their text, so that reading the chapter straight through makes sense. Do likewise when structuring the book into chapters, and when structuring a section into paragraphs. The watchword is, *at each point, address the most fundamental and important issue raised by the preceding text.*

If necessary, add extra chapters at the beginning of the manual which are purely tutorial and cover the basics of the subject. These provide the framework for a beginner to understand the rest of the manual. The Bison manual provides a good example of how to do this.

To serve as a reference, a manual should have an Index that lists all the functions, variables, options, and important concepts that are part of the program. One combined Index should do for a short manual, but sometimes for a complex package it is better to use multiple indices. The Texinfo manual includes advice on preparing good index entries, see Section "Making Index Entries" in *GNU Texinfo*, and see Section "Defining the Entries of an Index" in *GNU Texinfo*.

Don't use Unix man pages as a model for how to write GNU documentation; most of them are terse, badly structured, and give inadequate explanation of the underlying concepts. (There are, of course, some exceptions.) Also, Unix man pages use a particular format which is different from what we use in GNU manuals.

Please include an email address in the manual for where to report bugs *in the text of the manual.*

Please do not use the term "pathname" that is used in Unix documentation; use "file name" (two words) instead. We use the term "path" only for search paths, which are lists of directory names.

Please do not use the term "illegal" to refer to erroneous input to a computer program. Please use "invalid" for this, and reserve the term "illegal" for activities prohibited by law.

Please do not write '()' after a function name just to indicate it is a function. `foo ()` is not a function, it is a function call with no arguments.

6.2 Doc Strings and Manuals

Some programming systems, such as Emacs, provide a documentation string for each function, command or variable. You may be tempted to write a reference manual by compiling the documentation strings and writing a little additional text to go around them—but you must not do it. That approach is a fundamental mistake. The text of well-written documentation strings will be entirely wrong for a manual.

A documentation string needs to stand alone—when it appears on the screen, there will be no other text to introduce or explain it. Meanwhile, it can be rather informal in style.

The text describing a function or variable in a manual must not stand alone; it appears in the context of a section or subsection. Other text at the beginning of the section should explain some of the concepts, and should often make some general points that apply to several functions or variables. The previous descriptions of functions and variables in the section will also have given information about the topic. A description written to stand alone would repeat some of that information; this redundancy looks bad. Meanwhile, the informality that is acceptable in a documentation string is totally unacceptable in a manual.

The only good way to use documentation strings in writing a good manual is to use them as a source of information for writing good text.

6.3 Manual Structure Details

The title page of the manual should state the version of the programs or packages documented in the manual. The Top node of the manual should also contain this information. If the manual is changing more frequently than or independent of the program, also state a version number for the manual in both of these places.

Each program documented in the manual should have a node named '*program* Invocation' or 'Invoking *program*'. This node (together with its subnodes, if any) should describe the program's command line arguments and how to run it (the sort of information people would look for in a man page). Start with an '@example' containing a template for all the options and arguments that the program uses.

Alternatively, put a menu item in some menu whose item name fits one of the above patterns. This identifies the node which that item points to as the node for this purpose, regardless of the node's actual name.

The '--usage' feature of the Info reader looks for such a node or menu item in order to find the relevant text, so it is essential for every Texinfo file to have one.

If one manual describes several programs, it should have such a node for each program described in the manual.

6.4 License for Manuals

Please use the GNU Free Documentation License for all GNU manuals that are more than a few pages long. Likewise for a collection of short documents—you only need one copy of the GNU FDL for the whole collection. For a single short document, you can use a very permissive non-copyleft license, to avoid taking up space with a long license.

See `http://www.gnu.org/copyleft/fdl-howto.html` for more explanation of how to employ the GFDL.

Note that it is not obligatory to include a copy of the GNU GPL or GNU LGPL in a manual whose license is neither the GPL nor the LGPL. It can be a good idea to include the program's license in a large manual; in a short manual, whose size would be increased considerably by including the program's license, it is probably better not to include it.

6.5 Manual Credits

Please credit the principal human writers of the manual as the authors, on the title page of the manual. If a company sponsored the work, thank the company in a suitable place in the manual, but do not cite the company as an author.

6.6 Printed Manuals

The FSF publishes some GNU manuals in printed form. To encourage sales of these manuals, the on-line versions of the manual should mention at the very start that the printed manual is available and should point at information for getting it—for instance, with a link to the page `http://www.gnu.org/order/order.html`. This should not be included in the printed manual, though, because there it is redundant.

It is also useful to explain in the on-line forms of the manual how the user can print out the manual from the sources.

6.7 The NEWS File

In addition to its manual, the package should have a file named `NEWS` which contains a list of user-visible changes worth mentioning. In each new release, add items to the front of the file and identify the version they pertain to. Don't discard old items; leave them in the file after the newer items. This way, a user upgrading from any previous version can see what is new.

If the `NEWS` file gets very long, move some of the older items into a file named `ONEWS` and put a note at the end referring the user to that file.

6.8 Change Logs

Keep a change log to describe all the changes made to program source files. The purpose of this is so that people investigating bugs in the future will know about the changes that might have introduced the bug. Often a new bug can be found by looking at what was recently changed. More importantly, change logs can help you eliminate conceptual inconsistencies between different parts of a program, by giving you a history of how the conflicting concepts arose and who they came from.

6.8.1 Change Log Concepts

You can think of the change log as a conceptual "undo list" which explains how earlier versions were different from the current version. People can see the current version; they don't need the change log to tell them what is in it. What they want from a change log is a clear explanation of how the earlier version differed. Each *entry* in a change log describes either an individual change or the smallest batch of changes that belong together, also known as a *change set*. For later reference or for summarizing, sometimes it is useful to start the entry with a one-line description (sometimes called a *title*) to describe its overall purpose.

In the past, we recommended not mentioning changes in non-software files (manuals, help files, media files, etc.) in change logs. However, we've been advised that it is a good idea to include them, for the sake of copyright records.

The change log file is normally called `ChangeLog` and covers an entire directory. Each directory can have its own change log, or a directory can use the change log of its parent directory—it's up to you.

Another alternative is to record change log information with a version control system such as RCS or CVS. This can be converted automatically to a `ChangeLog` file using `rcs2log`; in Emacs, the command `C-x v a` (`vc-update-change-log`) does the job.

For changes to code, there's no need to describe the full purpose of the changes or how they work together. If you think that a change calls for explanation, you're probably right. Please do explain it—but please put the full explanation in comments in the code, where people will see it whenever they see the code. For example, "New function" is enough for the change log when you add a function, because there should be a comment before the function definition to explain what it does.

For changes to files that do not support a comment syntax (e.g., media files), it is ok to include the full explanation in the change log file, after the title and before the list of individual changes.

The easiest way to add an entry to `ChangeLog` is with the Emacs command *M-x add-change-log-entry*. An individual change should have an asterisk, the name of the changed file, and then in parentheses the name of the changed functions, variables or whatever, followed by a colon. Then describe the changes you made to that function or variable.

6.8.2 Style of Change Logs

Here are some simple examples of change log entries, starting with the header line that says who made the change and when it was installed, followed by descriptions of specific changes. (These examples are drawn from Emacs and GCC.)

```
1998-08-17  Richard Stallman  <rms@gnu.org>

* register.el (insert-register): Return nil.
(jump-to-register): Likewise.

* sort.el (sort-subr): Return nil.

* tex-mode.el (tex-bibtex-file, tex-file, tex-region):
Restart the tex shell if process is gone or stopped.
(tex-shell-running): New function.

* expr.c (store_one_arg): Round size up for move_block_to_reg.
(expand_call): Round up when emitting USE insns.
* stmt.c (assign_parms): Round size up for move_block_from_reg.
```

It's important to name the changed function or variable in full. Don't abbreviate function or variable names, and don't combine them. Subsequent maintainers will often search for a function name to find all the change log entries that pertain to it; if you abbreviate the name, they won't find it when they search.

For example, some people are tempted to abbreviate groups of function names by writing '`* register.el ({insert,jump-to}-register)`'; this is not a good idea, since searching for `jump-to-register` or `insert-register` would not find that entry.

Separate unrelated change log entries with blank lines. Don't put blank lines between individual changes of an entry. You can omit the file name and the asterisk when successive individual changes are in the same file.

Break long lists of function names by closing continued lines with ')', rather than ',', and opening the continuation with '(' as in this example:

```
* keyboard.c (menu_bar_items, tool_bar_items)
(Fexecute_extended_command): Deal with 'keymap' property.
```

When you install someone else's changes, put the contributor's name in the change log entry rather than in the text of the entry. In other words, write this:

```
2002-07-14  John Doe  <jdoe@gnu.org>

        * sewing.c: Make it sew.
```

rather than this:

```
2002-07-14  Usual Maintainer  <usual@gnu.org>

        * sewing.c: Make it sew.  Patch by jdoe@gnu.org.
```

As for the date, that should be the date you applied the change.

6.8.3 Simple Changes

Certain simple kinds of changes don't need much detail in the change log.

When you change the calling sequence of a function in a simple fashion, and you change all the callers of the function to use the new calling sequence, there is no need to make individual entries for all the callers that you changed. Just write in the entry for the function being called, "All callers changed"—like this:

```
* keyboard.c (Fcommand_execute): New arg SPECIAL.
All callers changed.
```

When you change just comments or doc strings, it is enough to write an entry for the file, without mentioning the functions. Just "Doc fixes" is enough for the change log.

There's no technical need to make change log entries for documentation files. This is because documentation is not susceptible to bugs that are hard to fix. Documentation does not consist of parts that must interact in a precisely engineered fashion. To correct an error, you need not know the history of the erroneous passage; it is enough to compare what the documentation says with the way the program actually works.

However, you should keep change logs for documentation files when the project gets copyright assignments from its contributors, so as to make the records of authorship more accurate.

6.8.4 Conditional Changes

Source files can often contain code that is conditional to build-time or static conditions. For example, C programs can contain compile-time `#if` conditionals; programs implemented in interpreted languages can contain module imports of function definitions that are only performed for certain versions of the interpreter; and Automake `Makefile.am` files can contain variable definitions or target declarations that are only to be considered if a configure-time Automake conditional is true.

Many changes are conditional as well: sometimes you add a new variable, or function, or even a new program or library, which is entirely dependent on a build-time condition. It is useful to indicate in the change log the conditions for which a change applies.

Our convention for indicating conditional changes is to use *square brackets around the name of the condition*.

Conditional changes can happen in numerous scenarios and with many variations, so here are some examples to help clarify. This first example describes changes in C, Perl, and Python files which are conditional but do not have an associated function or entity name:

```
* xterm.c [SOLARIS2]: Include <string.h>.
* FilePath.pm [$^O eq 'VMS']: Import the VMS::Feature module.
* framework.py [sys.version_info < (2, 6)]: Make "with" statement
  available by importing it from __future__,
  to support also python 2.5.
```

Our other examples will for simplicity be limited to C, as the minor changes necessary to adapt them to other languages should be self-evident.

Next, here is an entry describing a new definition which is entirely conditional: the C macro `FRAME_WINDOW_P` is defined (and used) only when the macro `HAVE_X_WINDOWS` is defined:

```
* frame.h [HAVE_X_WINDOWS] (FRAME_WINDOW_P): Macro defined.
```

Next, an entry for a change within the function `init_display`, whose definition as a whole is unconditional, but the changes themselves are contained in a '`#ifdef HAVE_LIBNCURSES`' conditional:

```
* dispnew.c (init_display) [HAVE_LIBNCURSES]: If X, call tgetent.
```

Finally, here is an entry for a change that takes effect only when a certain macro is *not* defined:

```
* host.c (gethostname) [!HAVE_SOCKETS]: Replace with winsock version.
```

6.8.5 Indicating the Part Changed

Indicate the part of a function which changed by using angle brackets enclosing an indication of what the changed part does. Here is an entry for a change in the part of the function `sh-while-getopts` that deals with `sh` commands:

```
* progmodes/sh-script.el (sh-while-getopts) <sh>: Handle case that
  user-specified option string is empty.
```

6.9 Man Pages

In the GNU project, man pages are secondary. It is not necessary or expected for every GNU program to have a man page, but some of them do. It's your choice whether to include a man page in your program.

When you make this decision, consider that supporting a man page requires continual effort each time the program is changed. The time you spend on the man page is time taken away from more useful work.

For a simple program which changes little, updating the man page may be a small job. Then there is little reason not to include a man page, if you have one.

For a large program that changes a great deal, updating a man page may be a substantial burden. If a user offers to donate a man page, you may find this gift costly to accept. It may be better to refuse the man page unless the same person agrees to take full responsibility for maintaining it—so that you can wash your hands of it entirely. If this volunteer later ceases to do the job, then don't feel obliged to pick it up yourself; it may be better to withdraw the man page from the distribution until someone else agrees to update it.

When a program changes only a little, you may feel that the discrepancies are small enough that the man page remains useful without updating. If so, put a prominent note near the beginning of the man page explaining that you don't maintain it and that the Texinfo manual is more authoritative. The note should say how to access the Texinfo documentation.

Be sure that man pages include a copyright statement and free license. The simple all-permissive license is appropriate for simple man pages (see Section "License Notices for Other Files" in *Information for GNU Maintainers*).

For long man pages, with enough explanation and documentation that they can be considered true manuals, use the GFDL (see Section 6.4 [License for Manuals], page 45).

Finally, the GNU help2man program (`http://www.gnu.org/software/help2man/`) is one way to automate generation of a man page, in this case from `--help` output. This is sufficient in many cases.

6.10 Reading other Manuals

There may be non-free books or documentation files that describe the program you are documenting.

It is ok to use these documents for reference, just as the author of a new algebra textbook can read other books on algebra. A large portion of any non-fiction book consists of facts, in this case facts about how a certain program works, and these facts are necessarily the same for everyone who writes about the subject. But be careful not to copy your outline structure, wording, tables or examples from preexisting non-free documentation. Copying from free documentation may be ok; please check with the FSF about the individual case.

7 The Release Process

Making a release is more than just bundling up your source files in a tar file and putting it up for FTP. You should set up your software so that it can be configured to run on a variety of systems. Your Makefile should conform to the GNU standards described below, and your directory layout should also conform to the standards discussed below. Doing so makes it easy to include your package into the larger framework of all GNU software.

7.1 How Configuration Should Work

Each GNU distribution should come with a shell script named `configure`. This script is given arguments which describe the kind of machine and system you want to compile the program for. The `configure` script must record the configuration options so that they affect compilation.

The description here is the specification of the interface for the `configure` script in GNU packages. Many packages implement it using GNU Autoconf (see Section "Introduction" in *Autoconf*) and/or GNU Automake (see Section "Introduction" in *Automake*), but you do not have to use these tools. You can implement it any way you like; for instance, by making `configure` be a wrapper around a completely different configuration system.

Another way for the `configure` script to operate is to make a link from a standard name such as `config.h` to the proper configuration file for the chosen system. If you use this technique, the distribution should *not* contain a file named `config.h`. This is so that people won't be able to build the program without configuring it first.

Another thing that `configure` can do is to edit the Makefile. If you do this, the distribution should *not* contain a file named `Makefile`. Instead, it should include a file `Makefile.in` which contains the input used for editing. Once again, this is so that people won't be able to build the program without configuring it first.

If `configure` does write the `Makefile`, then `Makefile` should have a target named `Makefile` which causes `configure` to be rerun, setting up the same configuration that was set up last time. The files that `configure` reads should be listed as dependencies of `Makefile`.

All the files which are output from the `configure` script should have comments at the beginning explaining that they were generated automatically using `configure`. This is so that users won't think of trying to edit them by hand.

The `configure` script should write a file named `config.status` which describes which configuration options were specified when the program was last configured. This file should be a shell script which, if run, will recreate the same configuration.

The `configure` script should accept an option of the form '`--srcdir=dirname`' to specify the directory where sources are found (if it is not the current directory). This makes it possible to build the program in a separate directory, so that the actual source directory is not modified.

If the user does not specify '`--srcdir`', then `configure` should check both . and .. to see if it can find the sources. If it finds the sources in one of these places, it should use them from there. Otherwise, it should report that it cannot find the sources, and should exit with nonzero status.

Usually the easy way to support '`--srcdir`' is by editing a definition of `VPATH` into the Makefile. Some rules may need to refer explicitly to the specified source directory. To make this possible, `configure` can add to the Makefile a variable named `srcdir` whose value is precisely the specified directory.

In addition, the 'configure' script should take options corresponding to most of the standard directory variables (see Section 7.2.5 [Directory Variables], page 57). Here is the list:

```
--prefix --exec-prefix --bindir --sbindir --libexecdir --sysconfdir
--sharedstatedir --localstatedir --runstatedir
--libdir --includedir --oldincludedir
--datarootdir --datadir --infodir --localedir --mandir --docdir
--htmldir --dvidir --pdfdir --psdir
```

The configure script should also take an argument which specifies the type of system to build the program for. This argument should look like this:

```
cpu-company-system
```

For example, an Athlon-based GNU/Linux system might be 'i686-pc-linux-gnu'.

The configure script needs to be able to decode all plausible alternatives for how to describe a machine. Thus, 'athlon-pc-gnu/linux' would be a valid alias. There is a shell script called config.sub (http://git.savannah.gnu.org/gitweb/?p=config.git;a=blob_plain;f=config.sub;hb=HEAD) that you can use as a subroutine to validate system types and canonicalize aliases.

The configure script should also take the option --build=*buildtype*, which should be equivalent to a plain *buildtype* argument. For example, 'configure --build=i686-pc-linux-gnu' is equivalent to 'configure i686-pc-linux-gnu'. When the build type is not specified by an option or argument, the configure script should normally guess it using the shell script config.guess (http://git.savannah.gnu.org/gitweb/?p=config.git;a=blob_plain;f=config.guess;hb=HEAD).

Other options are permitted to specify in more detail the software or hardware present on the machine, to include or exclude optional parts of the package, or to adjust the name of some tools or arguments to them:

'--enable-*feature*[=*parameter*]'

>   Configure the package to build and install an optional user-level facility called *feature*. This allows users to choose which optional features to include. Giving an optional *parameter* of 'no' should omit *feature*, if it is built by default.

>   No '--enable' option should **ever** cause one feature to replace another. No '--enable' option should ever substitute one useful behavior for another useful behavior. The only proper use for '--enable' is for questions of whether to build part of the program or exclude it.

'--with-*package*'

>   The package *package* will be installed, so configure this package to work with *package*.

>   Possible values of *package* include 'gnu-as' (or 'gas'), 'gnu-ld', 'gnu-libc', 'gdb', 'x', and 'x-toolkit'.

>   Do not use a '--with' option to specify the file name to use to find certain files. That is outside the scope of what '--with' options are for.

'*variable*=*value*'

>   Set the value of the variable *variable* to *value*. This is used to override the default values of commands or arguments in the build process. For example, the

> user could issue 'configure CFLAGS=-g CXXFLAGS=-g' to build with debugging information and without the default optimization.
>
> Specifying variables as arguments to configure, like this:
>
>   ./configure CC=gcc
>
> is preferable to setting them in environment variables:
>
>   CC=gcc ./configure
>
> as it helps to recreate the same configuration later with config.status. However, both methods should be supported.

All configure scripts should accept all of the "detail" options and the variable settings, whether or not they make any difference to the particular package at hand. In particular, they should accept any option that starts with '--with-' or '--enable-'. This is so users will be able to configure an entire GNU source tree at once with a single set of options.

You will note that the categories '--with-' and '--enable-' are narrow: they **do not** provide a place for any sort of option you might think of. That is deliberate. We want to limit the possible configuration options in GNU software. We do not want GNU programs to have idiosyncratic configuration options.

Packages that perform part of the compilation process may support cross-compilation. In such a case, the host and target machines for the program may be different.

The configure script should normally treat the specified type of system as both the host and the target, thus producing a program which works for the same type of machine that it runs on.

To compile a program to run on a host type that differs from the build type, use the configure option --host=*hosttype*, where *hosttype* uses the same syntax as *buildtype*. The host type normally defaults to the build type.

To configure a cross-compiler, cross-assembler, or what have you, you should specify a target different from the host, using the configure option '--target=*targettype*'. The syntax for *targettype* is the same as for the host type. So the command would look like this:

    ./configure --host=*hosttype* --target=*targettype*

The target type normally defaults to the host type. Programs for which cross-operation is not meaningful need not accept the '--target' option, because configuring an entire operating system for cross-operation is not a meaningful operation.

Some programs have ways of configuring themselves automatically. If your program is set up to do this, your configure script can simply ignore most of its arguments.

7.2 Makefile Conventions

This section describes conventions for writing the Makefiles for GNU programs. Using Automake will help you write a Makefile that follows these conventions. For more information on portable Makefiles, see POSIX and Section "Portable Make" in *Autoconf*.

7.2.1 General Conventions for Makefiles

Every Makefile should contain this line:

```
SHELL = /bin/sh
```

to avoid trouble on systems where the SHELL variable might be inherited from the environment. (This is never a problem with GNU make.)

Different make programs have incompatible suffix lists and implicit rules, and this sometimes creates confusion or misbehavior. So it is a good idea to set the suffix list explicitly using only the suffixes you need in the particular Makefile, like this:

```
.SUFFIXES:
.SUFFIXES: .c .o
```

The first line clears out the suffix list, the second introduces all suffixes which may be subject to implicit rules in this Makefile.

Don't assume that . is in the path for command execution. When you need to run programs that are a part of your package during the make, please make sure that it uses ./ if the program is built as part of the make or $(srcdir)/ if the file is an unchanging part of the source code. Without one of these prefixes, the current search path is used.

The distinction between ./ (the *build directory*) and $(srcdir)/ (the *source directory*) is important because users can build in a separate directory using the '--srcdir' option to configure. A rule of the form:

```
foo.1 : foo.man sedscript
        sed -f sedscript foo.man > foo.1
```

will fail when the build directory is not the source directory, because foo.man and sedscript are in the source directory.

When using GNU make, relying on 'VPATH' to find the source file will work in the case where there is a single dependency file, since the make automatic variable '$<' will represent the source file wherever it is. (Many versions of make set '$<' only in implicit rules.) A Makefile target like

```
foo.o : bar.c
        $(CC) -I. -I$(srcdir) $(CFLAGS) -c bar.c -o foo.o
```

should instead be written as

```
foo.o : bar.c
        $(CC) -I. -I$(srcdir) $(CFLAGS) -c $< -o $@
```

in order to allow 'VPATH' to work correctly. When the target has multiple dependencies, using an explicit '$(srcdir)' is the easiest way to make the rule work well. For example, the target above for foo.1 is best written as:

```
foo.1 : foo.man sedscript
        sed -f $(srcdir)/sedscript $(srcdir)/foo.man > $@
```

GNU distributions usually contain some files which are not source files—for example, Info files, and the output from Autoconf, Automake, Bison or Flex. Since these files normally appear in the source directory, they should always appear in the source directory, not in the build directory. So Makefile rules to update them should put the updated files in the source directory.

However, if a file does not appear in the distribution, then the Makefile should not put it in the source directory, because building a program in ordinary circumstances should not modify the source directory in any way.

Try to make the build and installation targets, at least (and all their subtargets) work correctly with a parallel make.

7.2.2 Utilities in Makefiles

Write the Makefile commands (and any shell scripts, such as `configure`) to run under `sh` (both the traditional Bourne shell and the POSIX shell), not `csh`. Don't use any special features of `ksh` or `bash`, or POSIX features not widely supported in traditional Bourne `sh`.

The `configure` script and the Makefile rules for building and installation should not use any utilities directly except these:

```
awk cat cmp cp diff echo egrep expr false grep install-info ln ls
mkdir mv printf pwd rm rmdir sed sleep sort tar test touch tr true
```

Compression programs such as `gzip` can be used in the `dist` rule.

Generally, stick to the widely-supported (usually POSIX-specified) options and features of these programs. For example, don't use 'mkdir -p', convenient as it may be, because a few systems don't support it at all and with others, it is not safe for parallel execution. For a list of known incompatibilities, see Section "Portable Shell" in *Autoconf*.

It is a good idea to avoid creating symbolic links in makefiles, since a few file systems don't support them.

The Makefile rules for building and installation can also use compilers and related programs, but should do so via `make` variables so that the user can substitute alternatives. Here are some of the programs we mean:

```
ar bison cc flex install ld ldconfig lex
make makeinfo ranlib texi2dvi yacc
```

Use the following `make` variables to run those programs:

```
$(AR) $(BISON) $(CC) $(FLEX) $(INSTALL) $(LD) $(LDCONFIG) $(LEX)
$(MAKE) $(MAKEINFO) $(RANLIB) $(TEXI2DVI) $(YACC)
```

When you use `ranlib` or `ldconfig`, you should make sure nothing bad happens if the system does not have the program in question. Arrange to ignore an error from that command, and print a message before the command to tell the user that failure of this command does not mean a problem. (The Autoconf 'AC_PROG_RANLIB' macro can help with this.)

If you use symbolic links, you should implement a fallback for systems that don't have symbolic links.

Additional utilities that can be used via Make variables are:

```
chgrp chmod chown mknod
```

It is ok to use other utilities in Makefile portions (or scripts) intended only for particular systems where you know those utilities exist.

7.2.3 Variables for Specifying Commands

Makefiles should provide variables for overriding certain commands, options, and so on.

In particular, you should run most utility programs via variables. Thus, if you use Bison, have a variable named `BISON` whose default value is set with 'BISON = bison', and refer to it with `$(BISON)` whenever you need to use Bison.

File management utilities such as `ln`, `rm`, `mv`, and so on, need not be referred to through variables in this way, since users don't need to replace them with other programs.

Each program-name variable should come with an options variable that is used to supply options to the program. Append 'FLAGS' to the program-name variable name to get the options variable name—for example, BISONFLAGS. (The names CFLAGS for the C compiler, YFLAGS for yacc, and LFLAGS for lex, are exceptions to this rule, but we keep them because they are standard.) Use CPPFLAGS in any compilation command that runs the preprocessor, and use LDFLAGS in any compilation command that does linking as well as in any direct use of ld.

If there are C compiler options that *must* be used for proper compilation of certain files, do not include them in CFLAGS. Users expect to be able to specify CFLAGS freely themselves. Instead, arrange to pass the necessary options to the C compiler independently of CFLAGS, by writing them explicitly in the compilation commands or by defining an implicit rule, like this:

```
CFLAGS = -g
ALL_CFLAGS = -I. $(CFLAGS)
.c.o:
        $(CC) -c $(CPPFLAGS) $(ALL_CFLAGS) $<
```

Do include the '-g' option in CFLAGS, because that is not *required* for proper compilation. You can consider it a default that is only recommended. If the package is set up so that it is compiled with GCC by default, then you might as well include '-O' in the default value of CFLAGS as well.

Put CFLAGS last in the compilation command, after other variables containing compiler options, so the user can use CFLAGS to override the others.

CFLAGS should be used in every invocation of the C compiler, both those which do compilation and those which do linking.

Every Makefile should define the variable INSTALL, which is the basic command for installing a file into the system.

Every Makefile should also define the variables INSTALL_PROGRAM and INSTALL_DATA. (The default for INSTALL_PROGRAM should be $(INSTALL); the default for INSTALL_DATA should be ${INSTALL} -m 644.) Then it should use those variables as the commands for actual installation, for executables and non-executables respectively. Minimal use of these variables is as follows:

```
$(INSTALL_PROGRAM) foo $(bindir)/foo
$(INSTALL_DATA) libfoo.a $(libdir)/libfoo.a
```

However, it is preferable to support a DESTDIR prefix on the target files, as explained in the next section.

It is acceptable, but not required, to install multiple files in one command, with the final argument being a directory, as in:

```
$(INSTALL_PROGRAM) foo bar baz $(bindir)
```

7.2.4 DESTDIR: Support for Staged Installs

DESTDIR is a variable prepended to each installed target file, like this:

```
$(INSTALL_PROGRAM) foo $(DESTDIR)$(bindir)/foo
$(INSTALL_DATA) libfoo.a $(DESTDIR)$(libdir)/libfoo.a
```

The DESTDIR variable is specified by the user on the make command line as an absolute file name. For example:

```
make DESTDIR=/tmp/stage install
```

DESTDIR should be supported only in the `install*` and `uninstall*` targets, as those are the only targets where it is useful.

If your installation step would normally install `/usr/local/bin/foo` and `/usr/local/lib/libfoo.a`, then an installation invoked as in the example above would install `/tmp/stage/usr/local/bin/foo` and `/tmp/stage/usr/local/lib/libfoo.a` instead.

Prepending the variable DESTDIR to each target in this way provides for *staged installs*, where the installed files are not placed directly into their expected location but are instead copied into a temporary location (`DESTDIR`). However, installed files maintain their relative directory structure and any embedded file names will not be modified.

You should not set the value of DESTDIR in your `Makefile` at all; then the files are installed into their expected locations by default. Also, specifying DESTDIR should not change the operation of the software in any way, so its value should not be included in any file contents.

DESTDIR support is commonly used in package creation. It is also helpful to users who want to understand what a given package will install where, and to allow users who don't normally have permissions to install into protected areas to build and install before gaining those permissions. Finally, it can be useful with tools such as `stow`, where code is installed in one place but made to appear to be installed somewhere else using symbolic links or special mount operations. So, we strongly recommend GNU packages support DESTDIR, though it is not an absolute requirement.

7.2.5 Variables for Installation Directories

Installation directories should always be named by variables, so it is easy to install in a nonstandard place. The standard names for these variables and the values they should have in GNU packages are described below. They are based on a standard file system layout; variants of it are used in GNU/Linux and other modern operating systems.

Installers are expected to override these values when calling make (e.g., *make prefix=/usr install*) or configure (e.g., *configure --prefix=/usr*). GNU packages should not try to guess which value should be appropriate for these variables on the system they are being installed onto: use the default settings specified here so that all GNU packages behave identically, allowing the installer to achieve any desired layout.

All installation directories, and their parent directories, should be created (if necessary) before they are installed into.

These first two variables set the root for the installation. All the other installation directories should be subdirectories of one of these two, and nothing should be directly installed into these two directories.

prefix   A prefix used in constructing the default values of the variables listed below. The default value of `prefix` should be `/usr/local`. When building the complete GNU system, the prefix will be empty and `/usr` will be a symbolic link to `/`. (If you are using Autoconf, write it as '`@prefix@`'.)

Running '`make install`' with a different value of `prefix` from the one used to build the program should *not* recompile the program.

`exec_prefix`

A prefix used in constructing the default values of some of the variables listed below. The default value of `exec_prefix` should be `$(prefix)`. (If you are using Autoconf, write it as '`@exec_prefix@`'.)

Generally, `$(exec_prefix)` is used for directories that contain machine-specific files (such as executables and subroutine libraries), while `$(prefix)` is used directly for other directories.

Running '`make install`' with a different value of `exec_prefix` from the one used to build the program should *not* recompile the program.

Executable programs are installed in one of the following directories.

`bindir`   The directory for installing executable programs that users can run. This should normally be `/usr/local/bin`, but write it as `$(exec_prefix)/bin`. (If you are using Autoconf, write it as '`@bindir@`'.)

`sbindir`   The directory for installing executable programs that can be run from the shell, but are only generally useful to system administrators. This should normally be `/usr/local/sbin`, but write it as `$(exec_prefix)/sbin`. (If you are using Autoconf, write it as '`@sbindir@`'.)

`libexecdir`

The directory for installing executable programs to be run by other programs rather than by users. This directory should normally be `/usr/local/libexec`, but write it as `$(exec_prefix)/libexec`. (If you are using Autoconf, write it as '`@libexecdir@`'.)

The definition of '`libexecdir`' is the same for all packages, so you should install your data in a subdirectory thereof. Most packages install their data under `$(libexecdir)/`*package-name*`/`, possibly within additional subdirectories thereof, such as `$(libexecdir)/`*package-name*`/`*machine*`/`*version*.

Data files used by the program during its execution are divided into categories in two ways.

- Some files are normally modified by programs; others are never normally modified (though users may edit some of these).
- Some files are architecture-independent and can be shared by all machines at a site; some are architecture-dependent and can be shared only by machines of the same kind and operating system; others may never be shared between two machines.

This makes for six different possibilities. However, we want to discourage the use of architecture-dependent files, aside from object files and libraries. It is much cleaner to make other data files architecture-independent, and it is generally not hard.

Here are the variables Makefiles should use to specify directories to put these various kinds of files in:

'`datarootdir`'

The root of the directory tree for read-only architecture-independent data files. This should normally be `/usr/local/share`, but write it as `$(prefix)/share`. (If you are using Autoconf, write it as '`@datarootdir@`'.) '`datadir`''s default value is based on this variable; so are '`infodir`', '`mandir`', and others.

'datadir'   The directory for installing idiosyncratic read-only architecture-independent data files for this program. This is usually the same place as 'datarootdir', but we use the two separate variables so that you can move these program-specific files without altering the location for Info files, man pages, etc.

This should normally be /usr/local/share, but write it as $(datarootdir). (If you are using Autoconf, write it as '@datadir@'.)

The definition of 'datadir' is the same for all packages, so you should install your data in a subdirectory thereof. Most packages install their data under $(datadir)/package-name/.

'sysconfdir'
The directory for installing read-only data files that pertain to a single machine—that is to say, files for configuring a host. Mailer and network configuration files, /etc/passwd, and so forth belong here. All the files in this directory should be ordinary ASCII text files. This directory should normally be /usr/local/etc, but write it as $(prefix)/etc. (If you are using Autoconf, write it as '@sysconfdir@'.)

Do not install executables here in this directory (they probably belong in $(libexecdir) or $(sbindir)). Also do not install files that are modified in the normal course of their use (programs whose purpose is to change the configuration of the system excluded). Those probably belong in $(localstatedir).

'sharedstatedir'
The directory for installing architecture-independent data files which the programs modify while they run. This should normally be /usr/local/com, but write it as $(prefix)/com. (If you are using Autoconf, write it as '@sharedstatedir@'.)

'localstatedir'
The directory for installing data files which the programs modify while they run, and that pertain to one specific machine. Users should never need to modify files in this directory to configure the package's operation; put such configuration information in separate files that go in $(datadir) or $(sysconfdir). $(localstatedir) should normally be /usr/local/var, but write it as $(prefix)/var. (If you are using Autoconf, write it as '@localstatedir@'.)

'runstatedir'
The directory for installing data files which the programs modify while they run, that pertain to one specific machine, and which need not persist longer than the execution of the program—which is generally long-lived, for example, until the next reboot. PID files for system daemons are a typical use. In addition, this directory should not be cleaned except perhaps at reboot, while the general /tmp (TMPDIR) may be cleaned arbitrarily. This should normally be /var/run, but write it as $(localstatedir)/run. Having it as a separate variable allows the use of /run if desired, for example. (If you are using Autoconf 2.70 or later, write it as '@runstatedir@'.)

These variables specify the directory for installing certain specific types of files, if your program has them. Every GNU package should have Info files, so every program needs 'infodir', but not all need 'libdir' or 'lispdir'.

'includedir'
: The directory for installing header files to be included by user programs with the C '#include' preprocessor directive. This should normally be /usr/local/include, but write it as $(prefix)/include. (If you are using Autoconf, write it as '@includedir@'.)

: Most compilers other than GCC do not look for header files in directory /usr/local/include. So installing the header files this way is only useful with GCC. Sometimes this is not a problem because some libraries are only really intended to work with GCC. But some libraries are intended to work with other compilers. They should install their header files in two places, one specified by includedir and one specified by oldincludedir.

'oldincludedir'
: The directory for installing '#include' header files for use with compilers other than GCC. This should normally be /usr/include. (If you are using Autoconf, you can write it as '@oldincludedir@'.)

: The Makefile commands should check whether the value of oldincludedir is empty. If it is, they should not try to use it; they should cancel the second installation of the header files.

: A package should not replace an existing header in this directory unless the header came from the same package. Thus, if your Foo package provides a header file foo.h, then it should install the header file in the oldincludedir directory if either (1) there is no foo.h there or (2) the foo.h that exists came from the Foo package.

: To tell whether foo.h came from the Foo package, put a magic string in the file—part of a comment—and grep for that string.

'docdir'
: The directory for installing documentation files (other than Info) for this package. By default, it should be /usr/local/share/doc/yourpkg, but it should be written as $(datarootdir)/doc/yourpkg. (If you are using Autoconf, write it as '@docdir@'.) The yourpkg subdirectory, which may include a version number, prevents collisions among files with common names, such as README.

'infodir'
: The directory for installing the Info files for this package. By default, it should be /usr/local/share/info, but it should be written as $(datarootdir)/info. (If you are using Autoconf, write it as '@infodir@'.) infodir is separate from docdir for compatibility with existing practice.

'htmldir'
'dvidir'
'pdfdir'
'psdir'
: Directories for installing documentation files in the particular format. They should all be set to $(docdir) by default. (If you are using Autoconf, write them as '@htmldir@', '@dvidir@', etc.) Packages which supply several

translations of their documentation should install them in '$(htmldir)/'*ll*, '$(pdfdir)/'*ll*, etc. where *ll* is a locale abbreviation such as 'en' or 'pt_BR'.

'libdir' The directory for object files and libraries of object code. Do not install executables here, they probably ought to go in $(libexecdir) instead. The value of libdir should normally be /usr/local/lib, but write it as $(exec_prefix)/lib. (If you are using Autoconf, write it as '@libdir@'.)

'lispdir' The directory for installing any Emacs Lisp files in this package. By default, it should be /usr/local/share/emacs/site-lisp, but it should be written as $(datarootdir)/emacs/site-lisp.

If you are using Autoconf, write the default as '@lispdir@'. In order to make '@lispdir@' work, you need the following lines in your configure.ac file:

```
lispdir='${datarootdir}/emacs/site-lisp'
AC_SUBST(lispdir)
```

'localedir'

The directory for installing locale-specific message catalogs for this package. By default, it should be /usr/local/share/locale, but it should be written as $(datarootdir)/locale. (If you are using Autoconf, write it as '@localedir@'.) This directory usually has a subdirectory per locale.

Unix-style man pages are installed in one of the following:

'mandir' The top-level directory for installing the man pages (if any) for this package. It will normally be /usr/local/share/man, but you should write it as $(datarootdir)/man. (If you are using Autoconf, write it as '@mandir@'.)

'man1dir' The directory for installing section 1 man pages. Write it as $(mandir)/man1.

'man2dir' The directory for installing section 2 man pages. Write it as $(mandir)/man2

'...'

Don't make the primary documentation for any GNU software be a man page. Write a manual in Texinfo instead. Man pages are just for the sake of people running GNU software on Unix, which is a secondary application only.

'manext' The file name extension for the installed man page. This should contain a period followed by the appropriate digit; it should normally be '.1'.

'man1ext' The file name extension for installed section 1 man pages.

'man2ext' The file name extension for installed section 2 man pages.

'...' Use these names instead of 'manext' if the package needs to install man pages in more than one section of the manual.

And finally, you should set the following variable:

'srcdir' The directory for the sources being compiled. The value of this variable is normally inserted by the configure shell script. (If you are using Autoconf, use 'srcdir = @srcdir@'.)

For example:

```
# Common prefix for installation directories.
# NOTE: This directory must exist when you start the install.
prefix = /usr/local
datarootdir = $(prefix)/share
datadir = $(datarootdir)
exec_prefix = $(prefix)
# Where to put the executable for the command 'gcc'.
bindir = $(exec_prefix)/bin
# Where to put the directories used by the compiler.
libexecdir = $(exec_prefix)/libexec
# Where to put the Info files.
infodir = $(datarootdir)/info
```

If your program installs a large number of files into one of the standard user-specified directories, it might be useful to group them into a subdirectory particular to that program. If you do this, you should write the `install` rule to create these subdirectories.

Do not expect the user to include the subdirectory name in the value of any of the variables listed above. The idea of having a uniform set of variable names for installation directories is to enable the user to specify the exact same values for several different GNU packages. In order for this to be useful, all the packages must be designed so that they will work sensibly when the user does so.

At times, not all of these variables may be implemented in the current release of Autoconf and/or Automake; but as of Autoconf 2.60, we believe all of them are. When any are missing, the descriptions here serve as specifications for what Autoconf will implement. As a programmer, you can either use a development version of Autoconf or avoid using these variables until a stable release is made which supports them.

7.2.6 Standard Targets for Users

All GNU programs should have the following targets in their Makefiles:

'all'   Compile the entire program. This should be the default target. This target need not rebuild any documentation files; Info files should normally be included in the distribution, and DVI (and other documentation format) files should be made only when explicitly asked for.

By default, the Make rules should compile and link with '-g', so that executable programs have debugging symbols. Otherwise, you are essentially helpless in the face of a crash, and it is often far from easy to reproduce with a fresh build.

'install'   Compile the program and copy the executables, libraries, and so on to the file names where they should reside for actual use. If there is a simple test to verify that a program is properly installed, this target should run that test.

Do not strip executables when installing them. This helps eventual debugging that may be needed later, and nowadays disk space is cheap and dynamic loaders typically ensure debug sections are not loaded during normal execution. Users that need stripped binaries may invoke the `install-strip` target to do that.

If possible, write the `install` target rule so that it does not modify anything in the directory where the program was built, provided 'make all' has just been done. This is convenient for building the program under one user name and installing it under another.

The commands should create all the directories in which files are to be installed, if they don't already exist. This includes the directories specified as the values of the variables `prefix` and `exec_prefix`, as well as all subdirectories that are needed. One way to do this is by means of an `installdirs` target as described below.

Use '-' before any command for installing a man page, so that `make` will ignore any errors. This is in case there are systems that don't have the Unix man page documentation system installed.

The way to install Info files is to copy them into `$(infodir)` with `$(INSTALL_DATA)` (see Section 7.2.3 [Command Variables], page 55), and then run the `install-info` program if it is present. `install-info` is a program that edits the Info `dir` file to add or update the menu entry for the given Info file; it is part of the Texinfo package.

Here is a sample rule to install an Info file that also tries to handle some additional situations, such as `install-info` not being present.

```
do-install-info: foo.info installdirs
        $(NORMAL_INSTALL)
# Prefer an info file in . to one in srcdir.
        if test -f foo.info; then d=.; \
         else d="$(srcdir)"; fi; \
        $(INSTALL_DATA) $$d/foo.info \
          "$(DESTDIR)$(infodir)/foo.info"
# Run install-info only if it exists.
# Use 'if' instead of just prepending '-' to the
# line so we notice real errors from install-info.
# Use '$(SHELL) -c' because some shells do not
# fail gracefully when there is an unknown command.
        $(POST_INSTALL)
        if $(SHELL) -c 'install-info --version' \
           >/dev/null 2>&1; then \
          install-info --dir-file="$(DESTDIR)$(infodir)/dir" \
                       "$(DESTDIR)$(infodir)/foo.info"; \
        else true; fi
```

When writing the `install` target, you must classify all the commands into three categories: normal ones, *pre-installation* commands and *post-installation* commands. See Section 7.2.7 [Install Command Categories], page 67.

'install-html'
'install-dvi'
'install-pdf'
'install-ps'

These targets install documentation in formats other than Info; they're intended to be called explicitly by the person installing the package, if that format is desired. GNU prefers Info files, so these must be installed by the `install` target.

When you have many documentation files to install, we recommend that you avoid collisions and clutter by arranging for these targets to install in subdirectories of the appropriate installation directory, such as `htmldir`. As one example, if your package has multiple manuals, and you wish to install HTML documentation with many files (such as the "split" mode output by `makeinfo`

--html), you'll certainly want to use subdirectories, or two nodes with the same name in different manuals will overwrite each other.

Please make these `install-format` targets invoke the commands for the *format* target, for example, by making *format* a dependency.

'uninstall'

Delete all the installed files—the copies that the 'install' and 'install-*' targets create.

This rule should not modify the directories where compilation is done, only the directories where files are installed.

The uninstallation commands are divided into three categories, just like the installation commands. See Section 7.2.7 [Install Command Categories], page 67.

'install-strip'

Like `install`, but strip the executable files while installing them. In simple cases, this target can use the `install` target in a simple way:

```
install-strip:
        $(MAKE) INSTALL_PROGRAM='$(INSTALL_PROGRAM) -s' \
                install
```

But if the package installs scripts as well as real executables, the `install-strip` target can't just refer to the `install` target; it has to strip the executables but not the scripts.

`install-strip` should not strip the executables in the build directory which are being copied for installation. It should only strip the copies that are installed.

Normally we do not recommend stripping an executable unless you are sure the program has no bugs. However, it can be reasonable to install a stripped executable for actual execution while saving the unstripped executable elsewhere in case there is a bug.

'clean'   Delete all files in the current directory that are normally created by building the program. Also delete files in other directories if they are created by this makefile. However, don't delete the files that record the configuration. Also preserve files that could be made by building, but normally aren't because the distribution comes with them. There is no need to delete parent directories that were created with 'mkdir -p', since they could have existed anyway.

Delete .dvi files here if they are not part of the distribution.

'distclean'

Delete all files in the current directory (or created by this makefile) that are created by configuring or building the program. If you have unpacked the source and built the program without creating any other files, 'make distclean' should leave only the files that were in the distribution. However, there is no need to delete parent directories that were created with 'mkdir -p', since they could have existed anyway.

'mostlyclean'

Like 'clean', but may refrain from deleting a few files that people normally don't want to recompile. For example, the 'mostlyclean' target for GCC does not delete `libgcc.a`, because recompiling it is rarely necessary and takes a lot of time.

`'maintainer-clean'`

Delete almost everything that can be reconstructed with this Makefile. This typically includes everything deleted by `distclean`, plus more: C source files produced by Bison, tags tables, Info files, and so on.

The reason we say "almost everything" is that running the command 'make maintainer-clean' should not delete `configure` even if `configure` can be re-made using a rule in the Makefile. More generally, 'make maintainer-clean' should not delete anything that needs to exist in order to run `configure` and then begin to build the program. Also, there is no need to delete parent directories that were created with 'mkdir -p', since they could have existed anyway. These are the only exceptions; `maintainer-clean` should delete everything else that can be rebuilt.

The 'maintainer-clean' target is intended to be used by a maintainer of the package, not by ordinary users. You may need special tools to reconstruct some of the files that 'make maintainer-clean' deletes. Since these files are normally included in the distribution, we don't take care to make them easy to reconstruct. If you find you need to unpack the full distribution again, don't blame us.

To help make users aware of this, the commands for the special `maintainer-clean` target should start with these two:

```
@echo 'This command is intended for maintainers to use; it'
@echo 'deletes files that may need special tools to rebuild.'
```

`'TAGS'`   Update a tags table for this program.

`'info'`   Generate any Info files needed. The best way to write the rules is as follows:

```
info: foo.info

foo.info: foo.texi chap1.texi chap2.texi
        $(MAKEINFO) $(srcdir)/foo.texi
```

You must define the variable `MAKEINFO` in the Makefile. It should run the `makeinfo` program, which is part of the Texinfo distribution.

Normally a GNU distribution comes with Info files, and that means the Info files are present in the source directory. Therefore, the Make rule for an info file should update it in the source directory. When users build the package, ordinarily Make will not update the Info files because they will already be up to date.

`'dvi'`
`'html'`
`'pdf'`
`'ps'`   Generate documentation files in the given format. These targets should always exist, but any or all can be a no-op if the given output format cannot be generated. These targets should not be dependencies of the `all` target; the user must manually invoke them.

Here's an example rule for generating DVI files from Texinfo:

```
dvi: foo.dvi

foo.dvi: foo.texi chap1.texi chap2.texi
        $(TEXI2DVI) $(srcdir)/foo.texi
```

You must define the variable TEXI2DVI in the Makefile. It should run the program texi2dvi, which is part of the Texinfo distribution. (texi2dvi uses TEX to do the real work of formatting. TEX is not distributed with Texinfo.) Alternatively, write only the dependencies, and allow GNU make to provide the command.

Here's another example, this one for generating HTML from Texinfo:

```
html: foo.html

foo.html: foo.texi chap1.texi chap2.texi
        $(TEXI2HTML) $(srcdir)/foo.texi
```

Again, you would define the variable TEXI2HTML in the Makefile; for example, it might run makeinfo --no-split --html (makeinfo is part of the Texinfo distribution).

'dist'
> Create a distribution tar file for this program. The tar file should be set up so that the file names in the tar file start with a subdirectory name which is the name of the package it is a distribution for. This name can include the version number.
>
> For example, the distribution tar file of GCC version 1.40 unpacks into a subdirectory named gcc-1.40.
>
> The easiest way to do this is to create a subdirectory appropriately named, use ln or cp to install the proper files in it, and then tar that subdirectory.
>
> Compress the tar file with gzip. For example, the actual distribution file for GCC version 1.40 is called gcc-1.40.tar.gz. It is ok to support other free compression formats as well.
>
> The dist target should explicitly depend on all non-source files that are in the distribution, to make sure they are up to date in the distribution. See Section 7.3 [Making Releases], page 68.

'check'
> Perform self-tests (if any). The user must build the program before running the tests, but need not install the program; you should write the self-tests so that they work when the program is built but not installed.

The following targets are suggested as conventional names, for programs in which they are useful.

installcheck
> Perform installation tests (if any). The user must build and install the program before running the tests. You should not assume that $(bindir) is in the search path.

installdirs
> It's useful to add a target named 'installdirs' to create the directories where files are installed, and their parent directories. There is a script called mkinstalldirs which is convenient for this; you can find it in the Gnulib package. You can use a rule like this:

```
# Make sure all installation directories (e.g. $(bindir))
# actually exist by making them if necessary.
installdirs: mkinstalldirs
        $(srcdir)/mkinstalldirs $(bindir) $(datadir) \
                                $(libdir) $(infodir) \
                                $(mandir)
```

or, if you wish to support DESTDIR (strongly encouraged),

```
# Make sure all installation directories (e.g. $(bindir))
# actually exist by making them if necessary.
installdirs: mkinstalldirs
        $(srcdir)/mkinstalldirs \
            $(DESTDIR)$(bindir) $(DESTDIR)$(datadir) \
            $(DESTDIR)$(libdir) $(DESTDIR)$(infodir) \
            $(DESTDIR)$(mandir)
```

This rule should not modify the directories where compilation is done. It should do nothing but create installation directories.

7.2.7 Install Command Categories

When writing the install target, you must classify all the commands into three categories: normal ones, *pre-installation* commands and *post-installation* commands.

Normal commands move files into their proper places, and set their modes. They may not alter any files except the ones that come entirely from the package they belong to.

Pre-installation and post-installation commands may alter other files; in particular, they can edit global configuration files or data bases.

Pre-installation commands are typically executed before the normal commands, and post-installation commands are typically run after the normal commands.

The most common use for a post-installation command is to run install-info. This cannot be done with a normal command, since it alters a file (the Info directory) which does not come entirely and solely from the package being installed. It is a post-installation command because it needs to be done after the normal command which installs the package's Info files.

Most programs don't need any pre-installation commands, but we have the feature just in case it is needed.

To classify the commands in the install rule into these three categories, insert *category lines* among them. A category line specifies the category for the commands that follow.

A category line consists of a tab and a reference to a special Make variable, plus an optional comment at the end. There are three variables you can use, one for each category; the variable name specifies the category. Category lines are no-ops in ordinary execution because these three Make variables are normally undefined (and you *should not* define them in the makefile).

Here are the three possible category lines, each with a comment that explains what it means:

```
$(PRE_INSTALL)      # Pre-install commands follow.
$(POST_INSTALL)     # Post-install commands follow.
$(NORMAL_INSTALL)   # Normal commands follow.
```

If you don't use a category line at the beginning of the install rule, all the commands are classified as normal until the first category line. If you don't use any category lines, all the commands are classified as normal.

These are the category lines for `uninstall`:

```
$(PRE_UNINSTALL)     # Pre-uninstall commands follow.
$(POST_UNINSTALL)    # Post-uninstall commands follow.
$(NORMAL_UNINSTALL)  # Normal commands follow.
```

Typically, a pre-uninstall command would be used for deleting entries from the Info directory.

If the `install` or `uninstall` target has any dependencies which act as subroutines of installation, then you should start *each* dependency's commands with a category line, and start the main target's commands with a category line also. This way, you can ensure that each command is placed in the right category regardless of which of the dependencies actually run.

Pre-installation and post-installation commands should not run any programs except for these:

```
[ basename bash cat chgrp chmod chown cmp cp dd diff echo
egrep expand expr false fgrep find getopt grep gunzip gzip
hostname install install-info kill ldconfig ln ls md5sum
mkdir mkfifo mknod mv printenv pwd rm rmdir sed sort tee
test touch true uname xargs yes
```

The reason for distinguishing the commands in this way is for the sake of making binary packages. Typically a binary package contains all the executables and other files that need to be installed, and has its own method of installing them—so it does not need to run the normal installation commands. But installing the binary package does need to execute the pre-installation and post-installation commands.

Programs to build binary packages work by extracting the pre-installation and post-installation commands. Here is one way of extracting the pre-installation commands (the `-s` option to `make` is needed to silence messages about entering subdirectories):

```
make -s -n install -o all \
      PRE_INSTALL=pre-install \
      POST_INSTALL=post-install \
      NORMAL_INSTALL=normal-install \
  | gawk -f pre-install.awk
```

where the file `pre-install.awk` could contain this:

```
$0 ~ /^(normal-install|post-install)[ \t]*$/ {on = 0}
on {print $0}
$0 ~ /^pre-install[ \t]*$/ {on = 1}
```

7.3 Making Releases

You should identify each release with a pair of version numbers, a major version and a minor. We have no objection to using more than two numbers, but it is very unlikely that you really need them.

Package the distribution of `Foo version 69.96` up in a gzipped tar file with the name `foo-69.96.tar.gz`. It should unpack into a subdirectory named `foo-69.96`.

Building and installing the program should never modify any of the files contained in the distribution. This means that all the files that form part of the program in any way must be classified into *source files* and *non-source files*. Source files are written by humans and never changed automatically; non-source files are produced from source files by programs under the control of the Makefile.

The distribution should contain a file named `README` with a general overview of the package:

- the name of the package;
- the version number of the package, or refer to where in the package the version can be found;
- a general description of what the package does;
- a reference to the file `INSTALL`, which should in turn contain an explanation of the installation procedure;
- a brief explanation of any unusual top-level directories or files, or other hints for readers to find their way around the source;
- a reference to the file which contains the copying conditions. The GNU GPL, if used, should be in a file called `COPYING`. If the GNU LGPL is used, it should be in a file called `COPYING.LESSER`.

Naturally, all the source files must be in the distribution. It is okay to include non-source files in the distribution along with the source files they are generated from, provided they are up-to-date with the source they are made from, and machine-independent, so that normal building of the distribution will never modify them. We commonly include non-source files produced by Autoconf, Automake, Bison, `flex`, TeX, and `makeinfo`; this helps avoid unnecessary dependencies between our distributions, so that users can install whichever versions of whichever packages they like. Do not induce new dependencies on other software lightly.

Non-source files that might actually be modified by building and installing the program should **never** be included in the distribution. So if you do distribute non-source files, always make sure they are up to date when you make a new distribution.

Make sure that all the files in the distribution are world-readable, and that directories are world-readable and world-searchable (octal mode 755). We used to recommend that all directories in the distribution also be world-writable (octal mode 777), because ancient versions of `tar` would otherwise not cope when extracting the archive as an unprivileged user. That can easily lead to security issues when creating the archive, however, so now we recommend against that.

Don't include any symbolic links in the distribution itself. If the tar file contains symbolic links, then people cannot even unpack it on systems that don't support symbolic links. Also, don't use multiple names for one file in different directories, because certain file systems cannot handle this and that prevents unpacking the distribution.

Try to make sure that all the file names will be unique on MS-DOS. A name on MS-DOS consists of up to 8 characters, optionally followed by a period and up to three characters. MS-DOS will truncate extra characters both before and after the period. Thus, `foobarhacker.c` and `foobarhacker.o` are not ambiguous; they are truncated to `foobarha.c` and `foobarha.o`, which are distinct.

Include in your distribution a copy of the `texinfo.tex` you used to test print any `*.texinfo` or `*.texi` files.

Likewise, if your program uses small GNU software packages like regex, getopt, obstack, or termcap, include them in the distribution file. Leaving them out would make the distribution file a little smaller at the expense of possible inconvenience to a user who doesn't know what other files to get.

8 References to Non-Free Software and Documentation

A GNU program should not recommend, promote, or grant legitimacy to the use of any non-free program. Proprietary software is a social and ethical problem, and our aim is to put an end to that problem. We can't stop some people from writing proprietary programs, or stop other people from using them, but we can and should refuse to advertise them to new potential customers, or to give the public the idea that their existence is ethical.

The GNU definition of free software is found on the GNU web site at `http://www.gnu.org/philosophy/free-sw.html`, and the definition of free documentation is found at `http://www.gnu.org/philosophy/free-doc.html`. The terms "free" and "non-free", used in this document, refer to those definitions.

A list of important licenses and whether they qualify as free is in `http://www.gnu.org/licenses/license-list.html`. If it is not clear whether a license qualifies as free, please ask the GNU Project by writing to `licensing@gnu.org`. We will answer, and if the license is an important one, we will add it to the list.

When a non-free program or system is well known, you can mention it in passing—that is harmless, since users who might want to use it probably already know about it. For instance, it is fine to explain how to build your package on top of some widely used non-free operating system, or how to use it together with some widely used non-free program.

However, you should give only the necessary information to help those who already use the non-free program to use your program with it—don't give, or refer to, any further information about the proprietary program, and don't imply that the proprietary program enhances your program, or that its existence is in any way a good thing. The goal should be that people already using the proprietary program will get the advice they need about how to use your free program with it, while people who don't already use the proprietary program will not see anything likely to lead them to take an interest in it.

If a non-free program or system is obscure in your program's domain, your program should not mention or support it at all, since doing so would tend to popularize the non-free program more than it popularizes your program. (You cannot hope to find many additional users for your program among the users of Foobar, if the existence of Foobar is not generally known among people who might want to use your program.)

Sometimes a program is free software in itself but depends on a non-free platform in order to run. For instance, many Java programs depend on some non-free Java libraries. To recommend or promote such a program is to promote the other programs it needs. This is why we are careful about listing Java programs in the Free Software Directory: we don't want to promote the non-free Java libraries.

We hope this particular problem with Java will be gone by and by, as we replace the remaining non-free standard Java libraries with free software, but the general principle will remain the same: don't recommend, promote or legitimize programs that depend on non-free software to run.

Some free programs strongly encourage the use of non-free software. A typical example is `mplayer`. It is free software in itself, and the free code can handle some kinds of files. However, `mplayer` recommends use of non-free codecs for other kinds of files, and users that install `mplayer` are very likely to install those codecs along with it. To recommend `mplayer` is, in effect, to promote use of the non-free codecs.

Thus, you should not recommend programs that strongly encourage the use of non-free software. This is why we do not list `mplayer` in the Free Software Directory.

A GNU package should not refer the user to any non-free documentation for free software. Free documentation that can be included in free operating systems is essential for completing the GNU system, or any free operating system, so encouraging it is a priority; to recommend use of documentation that we are not allowed to include undermines the impetus for the community to produce documentation that we can include. So GNU packages should never recommend non-free documentation.

By contrast, it is ok to refer to journal articles and textbooks in the comments of a program for explanation of how it functions, even though they are non-free. This is because we don't include such things in the GNU system even if they are free—they are outside the scope of what a software distribution needs to include.

Referring to a web site that describes or recommends a non-free program is promoting that program, so please do not make links to (or mention by name) web sites that contain such material. This policy is relevant particularly for the web pages for a GNU package.

Following links from nearly any web site can lead eventually to non-free software; this is inherent in the nature of the web. So it makes no sense to criticize a site for having such links. As long as the site does not itself recommend a non-free program, there is no need to consider the question of the sites that it links to for other reasons.

Thus, for example, you should not refer to AT&T's web site if that recommends AT&T's non-free software packages; you should not refer to a site that links to AT&T's site presenting it as a place to get some non-free program, because that link recommends and legitimizes the non-free program. However, that a site contains a link to AT&T's web site for some other purpose (such as long-distance telephone service) is not an objection against it.

Appendix A GNU Free Documentation License

Version 1.3, 3 November 2008

Copyright © 2000, 2001, 2002, 2007, 2008 Free Software Foundation, Inc.
`http://fsf.org/`

Everyone is permitted to copy and distribute verbatim copies
of this license document, but changing it is not allowed.

0. PREAMBLE

The purpose of this License is to make a manual, textbook, or other functional and useful document *free* in the sense of freedom: to assure everyone the effective freedom to copy and redistribute it, with or without modifying it, either commercially or non-commercially. Secondarily, this License preserves for the author and publisher a way to get credit for their work, while not being considered responsible for modifications made by others.

This License is a kind of "copyleft", which means that derivative works of the document must themselves be free in the same sense. It complements the GNU General Public License, which is a copyleft license designed for free software.

We have designed this License in order to use it for manuals for free software, because free software needs free documentation: a free program should come with manuals providing the same freedoms that the software does. But this License is not limited to software manuals; it can be used for any textual work, regardless of subject matter or whether it is published as a printed book. We recommend this License principally for works whose purpose is instruction or reference.

1. APPLICABILITY AND DEFINITIONS

This License applies to any manual or other work, in any medium, that contains a notice placed by the copyright holder saying it can be distributed under the terms of this License. Such a notice grants a world-wide, royalty-free license, unlimited in duration, to use that work under the conditions stated herein. The "Document", below, refers to any such manual or work. Any member of the public is a licensee, and is addressed as "you". You accept the license if you copy, modify or distribute the work in a way requiring permission under copyright law.

A "Modified Version" of the Document means any work containing the Document or a portion of it, either copied verbatim, or with modifications and/or translated into another language.

A "Secondary Section" is a named appendix or a front-matter section of the Document that deals exclusively with the relationship of the publishers or authors of the Document to the Document's overall subject (or to related matters) and contains nothing that could fall directly within that overall subject. (Thus, if the Document is in part a textbook of mathematics, a Secondary Section may not explain any mathematics.) The relationship could be a matter of historical connection with the subject or with related matters, or of legal, commercial, philosophical, ethical or political position regarding them.

The "Invariant Sections" are certain Secondary Sections whose titles are designated, as being those of Invariant Sections, in the notice that says that the Document is released under this License. If a section does not fit the above definition of Secondary then it is not allowed to be designated as Invariant. The Document may contain zero Invariant Sections. If the Document does not identify any Invariant Sections then there are none.

The "Cover Texts" are certain short passages of text that are listed, as Front-Cover Texts or Back-Cover Texts, in the notice that says that the Document is released under this License. A Front-Cover Text may be at most 5 words, and a Back-Cover Text may be at most 25 words.

A "Transparent" copy of the Document means a machine-readable copy, represented in a format whose specification is available to the general public, that is suitable for revising the document straightforwardly with generic text editors or (for images composed of pixels) generic paint programs or (for drawings) some widely available drawing editor, and that is suitable for input to text formatters or for automatic translation to a variety of formats suitable for input to text formatters. A copy made in an otherwise Transparent file format whose markup, or absence of markup, has been arranged to thwart or discourage subsequent modification by readers is not Transparent. An image format is not Transparent if used for any substantial amount of text. A copy that is not "Transparent" is called "Opaque".

Examples of suitable formats for Transparent copies include plain ASCII without markup, Texinfo input format, LaTeX input format, SGML or XML using a publicly available DTD, and standard-conforming simple HTML, PostScript or PDF designed for human modification. Examples of transparent image formats include PNG, XCF and JPG. Opaque formats include proprietary formats that can be read and edited only by proprietary word processors, SGML or XML for which the DTD and/or processing tools are not generally available, and the machine-generated HTML, PostScript or PDF produced by some word processors for output purposes only.

The "Title Page" means, for a printed book, the title page itself, plus such following pages as are needed to hold, legibly, the material this License requires to appear in the title page. For works in formats which do not have any title page as such, "Title Page" means the text near the most prominent appearance of the work's title, preceding the beginning of the body of the text.

The "publisher" means any person or entity that distributes copies of the Document to the public.

A section "Entitled XYZ" means a named subunit of the Document whose title either is precisely XYZ or contains XYZ in parentheses following text that translates XYZ in another language. (Here XYZ stands for a specific section name mentioned below, such as "Acknowledgements", "Dedications", "Endorsements", or "History".) To "Preserve the Title" of such a section when you modify the Document means that it remains a section "Entitled XYZ" according to this definition.

The Document may include Warranty Disclaimers next to the notice which states that this License applies to the Document. These Warranty Disclaimers are considered to be included by reference in this License, but only as regards disclaiming warranties: any other implication that these Warranty Disclaimers may have is void and has no effect on the meaning of this License.

2. VERBATIM COPYING

You may copy and distribute the Document in any medium, either commercially or noncommercially, provided that this License, the copyright notices, and the license notice saying this License applies to the Document are reproduced in all copies, and that you add no other conditions whatsoever to those of this License. You may not use technical measures to obstruct or control the reading or further copying of the copies you make or distribute. However, you may accept compensation in exchange for copies. If you distribute a large enough number of copies you must also follow the conditions in section 3.

You may also lend copies, under the same conditions stated above, and you may publicly display copies.

3. COPYING IN QUANTITY

If you publish printed copies (or copies in media that commonly have printed covers) of the Document, numbering more than 100, and the Document's license notice requires Cover Texts, you must enclose the copies in covers that carry, clearly and legibly, all these Cover Texts: Front-Cover Texts on the front cover, and Back-Cover Texts on the back cover. Both covers must also clearly and legibly identify you as the publisher of these copies. The front cover must present the full title with all words of the title equally prominent and visible. You may add other material on the covers in addition. Copying with changes limited to the covers, as long as they preserve the title of the Document and satisfy these conditions, can be treated as verbatim copying in other respects.

If the required texts for either cover are too voluminous to fit legibly, you should put the first ones listed (as many as fit reasonably) on the actual cover, and continue the rest onto adjacent pages.

If you publish or distribute Opaque copies of the Document numbering more than 100, you must either include a machine-readable Transparent copy along with each Opaque copy, or state in or with each Opaque copy a computer-network location from which the general network-using public has access to download using public-standard network protocols a complete Transparent copy of the Document, free of added material. If you use the latter option, you must take reasonably prudent steps, when you begin distribution of Opaque copies in quantity, to ensure that this Transparent copy will remain thus accessible at the stated location until at least one year after the last time you distribute an Opaque copy (directly or through your agents or retailers) of that edition to the public.

It is requested, but not required, that you contact the authors of the Document well before redistributing any large number of copies, to give them a chance to provide you with an updated version of the Document.

4. MODIFICATIONS

You may copy and distribute a Modified Version of the Document under the conditions of sections 2 and 3 above, provided that you release the Modified Version under precisely this License, with the Modified Version filling the role of the Document, thus licensing distribution and modification of the Modified Version to whoever possesses a copy of it. In addition, you must do these things in the Modified Version:

A. Use in the Title Page (and on the covers, if any) a title distinct from that of the Document, and from those of previous versions (which should, if there were any, be listed in the History section of the Document). You may use the same title as a previous version if the original publisher of that version gives permission.

B. List on the Title Page, as authors, one or more persons or entities responsible for authorship of the modifications in the Modified Version, together with at least five of the principal authors of the Document (all of its principal authors, if it has fewer than five), unless they release you from this requirement.

C. State on the Title page the name of the publisher of the Modified Version, as the publisher.

D. Preserve all the copyright notices of the Document.

E. Add an appropriate copyright notice for your modifications adjacent to the other copyright notices.

F. Include, immediately after the copyright notices, a license notice giving the public permission to use the Modified Version under the terms of this License, in the form shown in the Addendum below.

G. Preserve in that license notice the full lists of Invariant Sections and required Cover Texts given in the Document's license notice.

H. Include an unaltered copy of this License.

I. Preserve the section Entitled "History", Preserve its Title, and add to it an item stating at least the title, year, new authors, and publisher of the Modified Version as given on the Title Page. If there is no section Entitled "History" in the Document, create one stating the title, year, authors, and publisher of the Document as given on its Title Page, then add an item describing the Modified Version as stated in the previous sentence.

J. Preserve the network location, if any, given in the Document for public access to a Transparent copy of the Document, and likewise the network locations given in the Document for previous versions it was based on. These may be placed in the "History" section. You may omit a network location for a work that was published at least four years before the Document itself, or if the original publisher of the version it refers to gives permission.

K. For any section Entitled "Acknowledgements" or "Dedications", Preserve the Title of the section, and preserve in the section all the substance and tone of each of the contributor acknowledgements and/or dedications given therein.

L. Preserve all the Invariant Sections of the Document, unaltered in their text and in their titles. Section numbers or the equivalent are not considered part of the section titles.

M. Delete any section Entitled "Endorsements". Such a section may not be included in the Modified Version.

N. Do not retitle any existing section to be Entitled "Endorsements" or to conflict in title with any Invariant Section.

O. Preserve any Warranty Disclaimers.

If the Modified Version includes new front-matter sections or appendices that qualify as Secondary Sections and contain no material copied from the Document, you may at your option designate some or all of these sections as invariant. To do this, add their titles to the list of Invariant Sections in the Modified Version's license notice. These titles must be distinct from any other section titles.

You may add a section Entitled "Endorsements", provided it contains nothing but endorsements of your Modified Version by various parties—for example, statements of peer review or that the text has been approved by an organization as the authoritative definition of a standard.

You may add a passage of up to five words as a Front-Cover Text, and a passage of up to 25 words as a Back-Cover Text, to the end of the list of Cover Texts in the Modified Version. Only one passage of Front-Cover Text and one of Back-Cover Text may be added by (or through arrangements made by) any one entity. If the Document already includes a cover text for the same cover, previously added by you or by arrangement made by the same entity you are acting on behalf of, you may not add another; but you may replace the old one, on explicit permission from the previous publisher that added the old one.

The author(s) and publisher(s) of the Document do not by this License give permission to use their names for publicity for or to assert or imply endorsement of any Modified Version.

5. COMBINING DOCUMENTS

You may combine the Document with other documents released under this License, under the terms defined in section 4 above for modified versions, provided that you include in the combination all of the Invariant Sections of all of the original documents, unmodified, and list them all as Invariant Sections of your combined work in its license notice, and that you preserve all their Warranty Disclaimers.

The combined work need only contain one copy of this License, and multiple identical Invariant Sections may be replaced with a single copy. If there are multiple Invariant Sections with the same name but different contents, make the title of each such section unique by adding at the end of it, in parentheses, the name of the original author or publisher of that section if known, or else a unique number. Make the same adjustment to the section titles in the list of Invariant Sections in the license notice of the combined work.

In the combination, you must combine any sections Entitled "History" in the various original documents, forming one section Entitled "History"; likewise combine any sections Entitled "Acknowledgements", and any sections Entitled "Dedications". You must delete all sections Entitled "Endorsements."

6. COLLECTIONS OF DOCUMENTS

You may make a collection consisting of the Document and other documents released under this License, and replace the individual copies of this License in the various documents with a single copy that is included in the collection, provided that you follow the rules of this License for verbatim copying of each of the documents in all other respects.

You may extract a single document from such a collection, and distribute it individually under this License, provided you insert a copy of this License into the extracted document, and follow this License in all other respects regarding verbatim copying of that document.

7. AGGREGATION WITH INDEPENDENT WORKS

A compilation of the Document or its derivatives with other separate and independent documents or works, in or on a volume of a storage or distribution medium, is called an "aggregate" if the copyright resulting from the compilation is not used to limit the legal rights of the compilation's users beyond what the individual works permit. When the Document is included in an aggregate, this License does not apply to the other works in the aggregate which are not themselves derivative works of the Document.

If the Cover Text requirement of section 3 is applicable to these copies of the Document, then if the Document is less than one half of the entire aggregate, the Document's Cover Texts may be placed on covers that bracket the Document within the aggregate, or the electronic equivalent of covers if the Document is in electronic form. Otherwise they must appear on printed covers that bracket the whole aggregate.

8. TRANSLATION

Translation is considered a kind of modification, so you may distribute translations of the Document under the terms of section 4. Replacing Invariant Sections with translations requires special permission from their copyright holders, but you may include translations of some or all Invariant Sections in addition to the original versions of these Invariant Sections. You may include a translation of this License, and all the license notices in the Document, and any Warranty Disclaimers, provided that you also include the original English version of this License and the original versions of those notices and disclaimers. In case of a disagreement between the translation and the original version of this License or a notice or disclaimer, the original version will prevail.

If a section in the Document is Entitled "Acknowledgements", "Dedications", or "History", the requirement (section 4) to Preserve its Title (section 1) will typically require changing the actual title.

9. TERMINATION

You may not copy, modify, sublicense, or distribute the Document except as expressly provided under this License. Any attempt otherwise to copy, modify, sublicense, or distribute it is void, and will automatically terminate your rights under this License.

However, if you cease all violation of this License, then your license from a particular copyright holder is reinstated (a) provisionally, unless and until the copyright holder explicitly and finally terminates your license, and (b) permanently, if the copyright holder fails to notify you of the violation by some reasonable means prior to 60 days after the cessation.

Moreover, your license from a particular copyright holder is reinstated permanently if the copyright holder notifies you of the violation by some reasonable means, this is the first time you have received notice of violation of this License (for any work) from that copyright holder, and you cure the violation prior to 30 days after your receipt of the notice.

Termination of your rights under this section does not terminate the licenses of parties who have received copies or rights from you under this License. If your rights have been terminated and not permanently reinstated, receipt of a copy of some or all of the same material does not give you any rights to use it.

10. FUTURE REVISIONS OF THIS LICENSE

The Free Software Foundation may publish new, revised versions of the GNU Free Documentation License from time to time. Such new versions will be similar in spirit to the present version, but may differ in detail to address new problems or concerns. See http://www.gnu.org/copyleft/.

Each version of the License is given a distinguishing version number. If the Document specifies that a particular numbered version of this License "or any later version" applies to it, you have the option of following the terms and conditions either of that specified version or of any later version that has been published (not as a draft) by the Free Software Foundation. If the Document does not specify a version number of this License, you may choose any version ever published (not as a draft) by the Free Software Foundation. If the Document specifies that a proxy can decide which future versions of this License can be used, that proxy's public statement of acceptance of a version permanently authorizes you to choose that version for the Document.

11. RELICENSING

"Massive Multiauthor Collaboration Site" (or "MMC Site") means any World Wide Web server that publishes copyrightable works and also provides prominent facilities for anybody to edit those works. A public wiki that anybody can edit is an example of such a server. A "Massive Multiauthor Collaboration" (or "MMC") contained in the site means any set of copyrightable works thus published on the MMC site.

"CC-BY-SA" means the Creative Commons Attribution-Share Alike 3.0 license published by Creative Commons Corporation, a not-for-profit corporation with a principal place of business in San Francisco, California, as well as future copyleft versions of that license published by that same organization.

"Incorporate" means to publish or republish a Document, in whole or in part, as part of another Document.

An MMC is "eligible for relicensing" if it is licensed under this License, and if all works that were first published under this License somewhere other than this MMC, and subsequently incorporated in whole or in part into the MMC, (1) had no cover texts or invariant sections, and (2) were thus incorporated prior to November 1, 2008.

The operator of an MMC Site may republish an MMC contained in the site under CC-BY-SA on the same site at any time before August 1, 2009, provided the MMC is eligible for relicensing.

ADDENDUM: How to use this License for your documents

To use this License in a document you have written, include a copy of the License in the document and put the following copyright and license notices just after the title page:

```
Copyright (C) year your name.
Permission is granted to copy, distribute and/or modify this document
under the terms of the GNU Free Documentation License, Version 1.3
or any later version published by the Free Software Foundation;
with no Invariant Sections, no Front-Cover Texts, and no Back-Cover
Texts.  A copy of the license is included in the section entitled ''GNU
Free Documentation License''.
```

If you have Invariant Sections, Front-Cover Texts and Back-Cover Texts, replace the "with...Texts." line with this:

```
with the Invariant Sections being list their titles, with
the Front-Cover Texts being list, and with the Back-Cover Texts
being list.
```

If you have Invariant Sections without Cover Texts, or some other combination of the three, merge those two alternatives to suit the situation.

If your document contains nontrivial examples of program code, we recommend releasing these examples in parallel under your choice of free software license, such as the GNU General Public License, to permit their use in free software.

Index

www.ingramcontent.com/pod-product-compliance
Lightning Source LLC
LaVergne TN
LVHW080506080326
832902LV00045BB/2987